Helene

TRUE STORY OF A GERMAN GIRL'S RESILIENCE GROWING UP DURING WORLD WAR II

By HELGA LONG
and HELENE WITZMANN

ISBN: 978-1-943258-56-7

Edited by: Jessica Carelock

Published by Warren Publishing, Inc.
Charlotte, NC
www.warrenpublishing.net
Printed in the United States

Dedicated to my children and grandchildren.
May they be inspired by their grandmother's
and great-grandmother's positive attitude as they
face their own hardships throughout their lives.

ACKNOWLEDGEMENTS

As I bring this project to a close I realize that many people have helped me in this endeavor.

Those who read and edited the book include my daughter, Ashleigh Walsh, who surprised me with her knowledge of English grammar; Debbie Basinger, who has a wonderful way with words; Jill Morin, who took time out of her busy schedule to correct the many grammar mistakes; John Leslie, whose expertise in English and Literature was invaluable; and Scott Levin, who challenged me to become a better writer as I tried my hardest to meet his standards.

Those who helped me with computer skills, saving me hours of trial and error, are my daughter, Kristin Clement, my son-in-law, Todd Walsh, and my niece, Sarah Leslie, who provided the map of Germany for the book.

I also thank my brothers, Bernie and Frank Witzmann, for providing information and pictures, Inge Güsen for detailed family history, and Don Hughes, on whom I relied for correct historical data.

My biggest thanks goes out to my husband, Jim, who supported me all the way, and to whom I looked for good advice, encouragement, and finding typos.

RELEVANT AREAS OF GERMANY IN 1945

TABLE OF CONTENTS

INTRODUCTION

When families get together, oftentimes someone of the older generation begins to tell stories of the past. So was the case with my mother, Helene (Murmann) Witzmann. Her recollection of events that happened during her childhood, her teenage years during World War II, and surviving the war and its aftermath was remarkable. At one point, I realized that I should record her stories because they were too interesting to be forgotten. So, in 1995, we sat through recording sessions in her living room with audio tapes and a small tape recorder over many cups of coffee.

After twenty tapes had been filled, I let them lay in a shoe box in my office closet for fifteen years, too busy with my teaching career to translate the German narratives into what I regarded as a journal, written in English. When I finally began writing, this "journal" developed into a true story, a biography, about a typical German girl who felt the effects of the war and the Nazi regime; who grew into womanhood with the dangers of a war surrounding her; and who, through her positive nature, continued to live a challenging, yet happy life.

All of the events are represented as my mother remembered them. The reader may, at times, want more detail, but I did not want to "create" facts just to make the story sound more interesting. I did want to make sure that the historical events described were accurate, so I researched dates and times of bombings and attacks on various cities and found that her timeline was spot on.

I used some German terms which I italicized, followed by English explanations. German grammar requires that nouns be capitalized, so I kept the capitalization of those italicized nouns.

At the beginning of each chapter I've described the economic and political climate in Germany during the years which are covered in the chapter. I wanted to give context to events without delving into long, detailed aspects of World War II.

Whenever the topic is "World War II," the extermination of the Jewish people comes up. I asked my mother if she had known any Jewish people personally or had heard of the concentration camps. She answered that she was aware of a few Jewish store owners in Magdeburg and didn't learn of the concentration camps until after the war. As a child, she led a carefree life and had no interest in politics. By the time she was eighteen, she and many other Germans were just trying to exist. Their homes were destroyed. They were hungry and cold, and they had lost friends or family in the war. The changes in many parts of Germany were so gradual, that the average citizen gave no notice unless they were personally affected.

Helene's children and grandchildren have remarked over the years what an extraordinary woman she was with her ability to remain positive and to successfully handle the challenges that came her way. Having witnessed deprivation, suffering, and death, she made us aware of how trivial the things are that people today worry or get upset about. I learned from her not to put too much importance on material things; rather, to see and experience as much as possible in life. She said what is in your mind can never be taken away. Through her actions, she also taught us, that with hard work and perseverance, we could achieve any goal. We all feel blessed to have had such a wonderful mother and grandmother to look up to as a role model. I'm just proud to have been able to call her Mutti (Mom).

Helga Long

1
EARLY CHILDHOOD
SCHMÖLZ AND OSHERSLEBEN, 1925-1931

*I*n 1925, Germany was recovering from post–World War I
political turmoil and hyperinflation. The general public was
angry that Germany had lost land to France and Poland
through the Treaty of Versailles, and the older generation longed
for the pre-war monarchy of Kaiser Wilhelm II, when Germany
was economically prosperous and cultural life flourished. By
1928, the standard of living had been raised to pre-war level but
was followed by an economic depression in 1930, which caused
high unemployment nationwide. Small, rural communities
were less affected by the economic and political changes because
the farmers and local tradesmen were self-sufficient, raising
their own food and trading locally.

༄

I, Helene Murmann Witzmann, was born on January
11, 1925 in Schmölz, Oberfranken (Upper Franconia) in
Germany to Hans and Rosa (Scheler) Murmann. Schmölz
was a little village, and our small, white, stucco house was
that of my grandparents, where my parents were also living.
It was directly across the street from a pretty, tan colored,

stone church with a tall, slender steeple. I was born on a cold, wintry Sunday morning while the church bells were ringing. My mother said that the church bells' ringing was a very special sign and would hold special meaning. It meant that I would have good luck throughout my life.

As a baby, my health was very poor. When I was one year old I was very sick and the doctor could not figure out what was wrong. He finally had to say that it would do no good to come back for another house call. He could not help me. I was so weak that I could no longer be picked up in a normal way. I had to be picked up with a cloth or diaper used as a sling. But one day, a peddler came to the village and came to our door. It was a bitterly cold winter day so my mother let him into the house. He saw me lying on the table and my mother explained to him how sick and weak I was and how nothing had helped me get better. He said, "You know, Ma'am, I had a child that was very sick like that, and we gathered specific herbs. An old woman told us about these herbs that would help our child and where they grew, and they helped her get better." So my mother gathered the herbs, made a tea from them, and gave me a spoonful every hour until I was better. The next time the doctor came through the village, he said that he couldn't believe that I had survived.

I never got to know my grandparents because they died when I was a small child. I do know that my father's father was musically talented — he directed the church choir and was a wonderful violin player. He also distributed the church bulletins on Sunday mornings. On their way to church, people would stop by our house (since it was directly across the street from the church) and he would hand them out through the window.

I continued to be a weak child and small for my age, so my sisters, Elisabeth (two and a half years older than me) and Trudel (four years older than me) often pulled me around the streets in a little wagon. There was seldom traffic, especially in our small village. But one day, Trudel was hit by a car. She had received a new bicycle and was riding down the street, not paying attention to where she was going. Right after it happened, I saw the car sitting there with the mangled bicycle underneath it. My mother, crying, came running, and many other people also came running toward the accident. The people helped my mother get the bicycle and Trudel out from under the car. Other than a few bruises and scrapes, Trudel was not seriously hurt. Luckily, cars at that time did not travel very fast, were built higher, and the tires were small and narrow.

The people in the village were fairly poor. There were no big barns or homes, as some villages had. The village stretched along a valley with one main road running through, with meadows and small fields rising along both sides and low, wooded hills beyond. Besides the homes, there were a few small stores and several bars where the people gathered on an occasional evening or on the weekends to drink a beer or get something to eat. One of these bars had a dance every weekend for the young adults.

The people lived mainly on income earned from selling baskets made from vines found in the woods, whittled objects, or little boxes cut from bast. The boxes were used as storage for small items like crafts, handkerchiefs, and jewelry or as sewing boxes. My grandfather's and father's professions were basket weavers. They worked in a small shed behind the house. When they finished weaving a certain amount, they would strap on a big back-basket and walk or ride a bicycle to the bigger towns nearby to sell their wares.

In addition to this income, the family, as most others in the village, had some domestic animals. Beside the basket-weaving work shed there was another small shed for a couple of goats, several chickens, two sheep, some caged rabbits, and two cows. The cows not only provided milk, but also were used to pull a cart to the small fields that my grandfather owned outside the village where he grew potatoes, rye, wheat, and other vegetables to feed his family. It was often hard work for my grandparents, parents, my mother's older brother Georg Scheler (a master tailor), his wife Ida, and their four children because the rye and wheat had to be cut with sickles. For the children, it was fun to go out to the fields because we got to ride in the wagon. I always enjoyed that, although the cows often moved very slowly. Besides harvesting the crops in the fields, my aunt gathered many different types of herbs that grew wild, and she picked hazelnuts and apples from trees in their back yard. They had a big Kachelofen, a tile stove, in the living room on which she spread the nuts and dried them. There was also a small compartment in the stove where, in the fall, she would make baked apples that were always very delicious. Behind the house also stood a big brick oven where they baked bread once a week. Various mushrooms, found in the surrounding woods, also added to our diet, as well as blueberries (*Heidelbeeren*) and cranberries.

Another uncle, my mother's younger brother Adam Scheler, who lived in Bad Nauheim, was also a master tailor. He and his wife, Leni, were my godparents. (The name, Leni, is a short version of Helene. I, too, went by the name,

Leni.) He recognized that my father was a smart young man but that there were no opportunities to advance in life in such a small, modest village. He said to my father, "Hans, the best thing for you would be that you get out of Schmölz and learn a trade". So, my mother stayed there with us children and my father went to Bad Nauheim and learned the restaurant and hotel management business. He occasionally sent my mother money during this time. The training lasted a couple of years, but when he was finished, in 1930 when I was five years old, we were able to move away from Schmölz.

My father found a position in Oschersleben, on the Bode River, not far from the Harz Mountains. He took over the management position at a *Gasthof* (an inn) from an elderly couple who could no longer keep up with the demands of running an inn. He found an apartment and then sent for us. This apartment was located above a car dealership. It was a new building and the store below was big with many cars being displayed. There was a second part of the store beside it that remained vacant. Although the store owner did not have children of his own, he took a liking to us and gave us presents every now and then. One year, at Easter time, he hid Easter eggs and chocolate bunnies in the vacant part: behind posts, on ceiling beams, and on window sills. Because I was the smallest and couldn't always see the higher hidden eggs very well, he lifted me up and carried me around so that I could find my share. He also gave us chocolate rabbits.

In Oschersleben I went to the "kindergarten," which I really enjoyed. They had a tradition that when a new student arrived, there was a little celebration with candles, and I felt that I was being specially honored. Also, when I had to leave, they had a farewell party for me. My sisters did not fare as well. They were old enough to go to the elementary school and were laughed at because they spoke with an Upper-Franconian dialect, similar to the Bavarian dialect. They could not change their pronunciation but I was still young enough that I had no problems speaking the local dialect. After some time, they did become friends with the daughters of the local veterinarian.

2

MIDDLE
CHILDHOOD YEARS
GRÖNINGEN, 1931-1936

During these years, all aspects of life in Germany changed. The depression of 1930 caused middle-class Germans to lose confidence in the economy and the government, and increasing numbers of workers shifted their allegiance to either the Communist Party or to the Nazi Party. In 1933, because of the instability of the government, Adolf Hitler came into power. He gained the respect of many Germans by decreasing unemployment, giving farmers ownership of their fields, promising big improvements in the infrastructure, and giving speeches including continuous assurances of peace. He also began his anti-Jewish campaign with little resistance. Many who were aware of this thought it was just a temporary measure.

꘎

We only lived in Oschersleben a year. My father then found a small hotel, Hotel zum Kronprinzen, in Gröningen that he could rent and manage. It had guest rooms as well as a little restaurant and was situated between two streets: a main street at the front of the hotel and a small back street, from which you had access to the back entrance. The back street was named *Grabenstraße* (Graben Street) because a deep ditch (*Graben*) ran along the street. There was also a small bridge that led to our rear entrance. The main street was always very busy with traffic coming from Halberstadt, Magdeburg, and even Berlin. The street made a sharp right turn at our hotel. My friends and I often sat on our front steps and played a game we called, "The next car is mine." It was fun and exciting as we competed to see who could collect the most shiny, luxurious cars and who ended up with the most dull clunkers. The main building contained not only the hotel, but also a post office with an apartment for the postmaster and his family on the second floor. The guest rooms on the second floor of the hotel extended across an arch through which you could enter the inner court yard. We also had some stables because at that time not everyone had cars and some still traveled by horse and buggy. The restaurant kitchen was large, and in one corner underneath a window sat a large table with benches built into the corner walls. This was where my sisters and I spent much of our time in the coming years doing our homework.

Gröningen had the second biggest sugar factory in Germany. Despite this big factory, the town still had the qualities of a small, rural village. There was no water line, so homes did not have running water. We had a well outside in our courtyard with a pipe that ran into the kitchen. With the well in place we did have running water there through a little pump, but the guest rooms in the hotel all had china pitchers, wash bowls, and chamber pots. There were two public fountains on the main street where the women went to get their drinking water. They used a shoulder harness from which two buckets hung at either end. Because the water from our well was hard with minerals, my sisters and I had to fetch water from the Bode River whenever my mother needed to do laundry. To do this, we pulled a tank that was secured on a wagon to the river and climbed down and up the steep banks with our buckets until the tank was filled. Since I was still little, my sisters had to lug the water up from the river, and all I had to do was help push the wagon back home. When we were back home, the water was poured into a big kettle, under which a fire was built to heat the water and the laundry was boiled. Then it went into a large agitator-type wash machine with ringers to squeeze out the water. The wash machine was run by electricity. That is how my mother washed all the linens from the hotel.

While in Gröningen, I started elementary school, Volksschule. School began at 7:00 a.m. except in the winter months, when it began at 8:00 a.m. I walked to school and always carried a small bag which hung from my shoulder and contained a sandwich and an apple or a pickle. During class, the boys sat on long benches on one side of the room and the girls sat on the other, with a desk-table in front of us. The first thing we did to begin the school day was sing a hymn and say a prayer. Sometimes this was followed with a song that celebrated a special holiday, like Christmas, Easter, or May Day. Then our lessons began. As first graders, we wrote on small, individual black boards. One side had lines to practice writing since neatness was very important and continually stressed, and the other side of the board had a grid to practice numbers and math. We also had to memorize multiplication tables. All the other subjects were gradually added as we progressed. After each lesson, we had a short break with enough time to use the bathroom or just get up and stretch. We also had two longer, fifteen minute breaks, where we went outside into the school courtyard if the weather permitted and ate our sandwiches, talked with friends, or went for a stroll. It wasn't like a recess where everyone played or rough-housed. A teacher was always on duty to ensure that students behaved themselves.

The teachers were very strict. Besides getting spanked with a rod, students could also get their ears pulled or their faces slapped. In the first grade, I had a teacher who would smack our hands with a rod if we moved our fingers on the desk instead of keeping our hands quiet. Since I couldn't sit still for one minute, that posed a real problem for me! One incident that taught me a lesson was when I played with my new pencil box while the teacher was talking. The pretty little box was a gift for the start of the first grade from my god parents that held pencils, chalk, and a small sponge used to clean off my individual little blackboard. I was tempted into lifting the lid and letting it snap back when suddenly I felt a crack across my fingers, caused by the striking rod. I had red streaks across by fingers that burned painfully.

In the second grade, we had a music teacher who had lost a leg in World War I. He had a wooden leg and used a walking stick to get around. He also used the stick to punish his students. If something was amiss, he struck the student on the back or on the butt. Fortunately, he punished boys more in this way than girls. Our parents didn't seem to mind. In fact, when someone snitched on me that I had gotten "the stick", I received another spanking at home. This was just the way things were, and we didn't hold this against him. He organized a wooden flute music choir where every student in the class bought a wooden flute (like the recorders in the U.S.). Some were large bass flutes. This was so much fun for all of us and sounded so good that we gave concerts for the parents on various occasions.

I especially enjoyed the music classes, physical education, and hiking days. In the music classes, we enjoyed learning and singing new songs, in addition to playing the flutes. In the physical education classes, *Leibesübungen*, we played with big medicine balls, did some tumbling on mats, learned rope climbing and rope skipping, had relay races, and played team games. The *Wandertage* (hiking days) were days where the class hiked into the Harz forest. There were playgrounds along the hiking trails or areas where we would stop and spend more time. We often presented plays in these areas, usually a favorite fairy tale. We knew them all by heart. Those students who weren't interested in acting were our audience.

In the winter, when the local lake, Der Luther See, was frozen over, the entire school was given the day off to go ice skating. There were bonfires set along the banks, everyone brought something to eat, and it was great fun for the entire school to spend the afternoon ice skating. Cattails grew along part of the bank. Some of the boys cut these off, lit, and smoked them like cigars, and some actually got sick from that. We girls thought that was really funny.

There was also a small Catholic school in our town. The Catholics and the Protestants were not friendly with each other, and therefore the children were also antagonistic toward each other. I was always afraid of the Catholic children and thought it must be terrible to be a Catholic.

My sisters and I took piano lessons, each from a different teacher. Trudel's teacher was also Elisabeth's music teacher at her middle school. He had a reputation for being brutal in his punishment. One day, Elisabeth came home from school crying. She was an exceptionally good student who always did her best in her school work. The music teacher hadn't liked something about her work and had severely punched her in the back. It left such a nasty bruise that my father took her to the doctor to have her examined. The doctor reported the teacher to the authorities and he was given a warning that he would lose his job if this ever happened again. Because of this teacher's abhorrent behavior, Trudel quit taking lessons with him. Elisabeth took her lessons from my school music teacher (the one with the wooden flutes) and I took lessons from the music teacher from the dreaded Catholic school. He was a very nice man but lived on the second floor of the school building, so I had to go to that building to take my lessons with him. I was always fearful of having to do that. One time, as I approached the building, several boys who were playing in the gravel school yard began to throw stones at me. It hurt, and I was so scared that I stood frozen in place and began crying loudly, tears streaming down my face. The teacher heard me from his window. He ran down and yelled at the boys and chased them away, and then he comforted me. He said that he would always watch for me from his window, and there were no more incidences after that.

We wore the same dress to school for a long time until it needed to be washed, but we wore a simple apron over it and that was changed more often. These aprons were often embroidered and we were especially proud when we were old enough to embroider our own aprons and show them off at school. A hand-embroidered apron also became a nice birthday gift for a friend. Most mothers stayed at home, so much of the clothing was home-sewn. All the girls also crocheted and knitted. For winter we knitted warm, colorful, woolen socks. When we wore our high boots that laced up the front, we folded the socks over the tops of the boots. A pair of socks was also a popular birthday gift, as were knitted gloves, scarves, and caps, often matching.

My mother, although busy all day, usually was knitting something in the evening. One time she knitted each of us girls a beautiful, red collared sweater with a special pattern in it that we wore with black pleated skirts and long, black knitted stockings. They were beautiful, stylish outfits. In those days girls did not wear slacks but did wear long knitted stockings in the winter.

The only pants that you would see girls wearing were ski pants. We didn't own actual ski pants but wore sweatpants over our socks with our skirts tucked in, along with a jacket, gloves, cap, and scarf; all which kept us warm. There was a hill outside Gröningen near the Grabenstraße with a cemetery at the top. It was a great sledding hill, you just had to be careful not to hit the ditch that ran along the road. We would spend entire afternoons sledding. It was so much fun that we didn't think about how many times we climbed up the hill after sledding down. We first realized how cold, wet, and tired we were when dusk approached, and we had to walk home. There were many times when I opened our house door, fell into my mother's loving arms, and just bawled, I was so spent.

We often went ice skating too, but I wasn't very good at that. The skates we used consisted of a contoured metal plate with a blade underneath that stuck onto the bottom of your boot or shoe. A key then helped tighten the plate for a better hold. The skates that were boots with attached blades were only for the rich or the professionals.

⋐≈✦≈⋑

I had many friends in Gröningen. My parents were very busy with the hotel and restaurant and couldn't spend much time with me, but they encouraged me to have friends from some of the higher-class families in the community so that I would learn the educated German rather than the local dialect. Anita, whose father worked for the sugar factory, lived in an apartment above a store in the Grabenstraße, near enough for us to play together often. Another friend, Martha, whose father was the chief of police, lived on the outskirts of town. They had a very nice home with a big yard and garden where I helped pick strawberries, gooseberries, or whatever was in season. I particularly loved the yard because all we had was a small stone courtyard.

The daughter of the local veterinarian, Othelia Güroll, wasn't one of my favorite friends, but I played with her every Sunday afternoon. I just didn't like her as much as my other friends. Her father came to our restaurant on Sunday afternoons to get several buckets of ice to make ice cream. (My father had large blocks of ice delivered that were kept in the basement to cool the beer kegs and keep the meat from spoiling.) Then Othelia's father took me back home with him. I had fun playing in their large, beautiful yard and eating meringue balls that were cut in halves and filled with the ice cream. One summer afternoon, there was lots of excitement. On the radio we heard that the Graf Zeppelin, the famous passenger-carrying, hydrogen-filled airship, was going to be flying over Gröningen. This was something totally new for us. On that afternoon, the Güroll family and their maids and I climbed up a tall ladder onto one of the buildings used to house the animals from the veterinarian practice. We could see other people on other neighboring rooftops. As the Zeppelin passed over, we all waved wildly. One girl even took off her blouse and waved it.

Another friend, Inge, and her younger sisters loved to play with me. Their father was the proprietor of much land and they and their grandparents lived in the castle of the Gröningen cloister. The mother was very active in the community. She had organized a youth group that met in one of their buildings near the castle and at times they performed a play, for which she made all the costumes. They would walk me from the hotel to their home where we would play in their large, well equipped children's room. In the afternoon, we were required to join the parents for coffee time, although we children drank milk. It was very formal. A stone balcony stretched along the south side of the castle. The entire outside wall of the long room that faced south contained windows and French doors that opened to this balcony. This was the first thing you saw when you entered the castle. To me it looked amazing. The floor was wooden, and all kinds of taxidermized animals were displayed throughout the room: exotic birds, wild boars, deer, and other animals.

Inge desperately wanted me to come to her eighth birthday party, so she and her parents walked to the hotel to pick me up to make sure that I would be there. I wore my prettiest dress. When we neared the castle, we could already see many horses, buggies, and cars driving up to the castle to deliver their children. First, we children played tag and hide-and-seek outside until everyone had arrived. Then we were called to line up and enter the castle one by one. When we entered, another surprise awaited us. All of the servants were dressed up as characters from fairy tales, in costumes sewn by the mother. She herself stood by the door as we entered, dressed in a beautiful gown, and gave each of us a purse made of paper that contained play money. We were then led to the children's room where all the furniture had been removed and play stations had been set up to represent a carnival atmosphere. We could use our play money to play games of chance and win small gifts or buy cookies and little cakes. After we had played for some time, another room was opened to us. It was darkened, music began to play, and Inge and her little sisters performed a ballet for their guests. What a wonderful birthday party that was!

I was only eight and couldn't help in the hotel as my sisters did, so I was left to entertain myself. I would often walk to a friend's house only to find that they had to help in the vegetable garden, so I would ask if I could help, too. The answer was always, "Of course," so I enjoyed pulling weeds or picking up potatoes others had dug up with my friend. The parents often gave me a few coins for my help, which made me happy. Sometimes, friends came to my home and we played a game where you bounced a ball against an outside wall in various ways without it dropping. On rainy days, we could even play this within the thick walls of the arched doorway that led into our inner courtyard. There was a beam that stretched across the top of the arch, and each year a swallow built a nest on it where we could see it. We really enjoyed watching when the baby birds were old enough to be fed by the mother. We spent a lot of time quietly sitting on the stone pavement, watching as the mother bird flew in and stuffed food into the hungry little beaks. Sometimes my friends brought extra clothes along and we planned, practiced, and then performed a play for whomever would be willing to watch. We just pretended to be a certain character, using old curtains to become a bride, for instance.

In my younger years, we still played with dolls and my friends and I would meet with our dolls and strollers and stroll down the street like the adult mothers would do, or we would set up an area within the courtyard and play "house". We used our imaginations a lot. Hide-and-seek and tag were also games we enjoyed playing. The street behind our house had a short stretch that was cemented and was smooth enough to spin a top. To do this you had to tightly wind a whip around the top and give it a strong pull to get it started. Then you kept it spinning by gently "whipping" it. Sometimes we competed with friends to see who could keep theirs spinning the longest. The yoyo also started as a fad and we enjoyed doing all kinds of tricks with it. If the weather was too nasty to play outside, we got together at someone's home and played board games, word games, or card games. We also loved to read. I read the *Goldköpchen* series (Goldilocks, about a girl with blonde curls), *Die Nesteckchen* books (which took place during World War I), and Wilhelm Busch books.

At that time, a new mayor was assigned to Gröningen. One afternoon while sitting in our restaurant, enjoying a beer, he saw me and asked my name and how old I was. He said that he had a daughter one year younger who hadn't met anyone her age yet and didn't have anyone to play with. He asked if I would be willing to come to their house and play with her. I agreed to go on the next afternoon and he gave me directions. The next day I walked to their house, which was pretty with a flower garden in the front and in the back. Her name was Ute Marie Urbahn and she was a pretty little girl with big brown eyes and long brown hair with a big bow on the side. We enjoyed playing with each other and found that we had many of the same interests. I went frequently after that to play with her, but I also had my other friends with whom I liked to play. Sometimes they would call on the phone, and that was a new experience for me, as I had never been able to use the phone. It was one of those phones in a big wooden box high on the wall so that I couldn't even reach it. If you wanted to call out, you had to turn the crank, give the number to an operator, and wait to be connected.

≈≈≈

My parents didn't actually have their own living quarters, so our lives revolved pretty much around the hotel and restaurant. This had some advantages because we were able to interact more and meet some of the interesting guests who stayed there. We also had to be on our best behavior to reflect well on the hotel. Our most frequent guests were the truck drivers who drove semi-trucks to and from the sugar factory. Their routine was that they would drive their empty trucks to the sugar factory, leave the trailer to be loaded during the night, and park the cab part of the truck behind our hotel. They always used our hotel to stay overnight. They had their evening meal with us and then breakfast before they left again. The reason they enjoyed staying at our hotel was that most of them were from Bavaria, some even wearing their Lederhosen. Of course, since my parents were also from the upper Bavaria area, they spoke the Bavarian dialect and were able to understand each other. They enjoyed my mother's home cooking. I usually couldn't wait until they could come again because they were always so nice to me and many times gave me chocolates. One time, one of the truck drivers had to stay over on the weekend because his trailer could not be filled, so he said to us girls, "I'll drive you all to the Harz Mountains in my cab". And he did! We all easily fit into that large cab, but what a scary drive it was for me. First of all, we sat very high, and it seemed like we were going faster than normal, too fast around the curves, and then the roads became even steeper and curvier. I thought we weren't going to make it! While in the mountains we stopped at a place where you could buy food and enjoy a beautiful view. It also had a playground. He bought us each an ice cream cone and a lemonade, and I enjoyed playing on the playground. Then we headed back home.

In 1933, when I was eight years old, Adolf Hitler was gaining power. It was election day and all the adults had to vote. My parents did not mention for whom they voted. As a child, I had no interest in politics, but I sensed that my father did not like Hitler. Schools were closed on that day because voting took place in the schools. Businesses were also closed. We children stood outside and watched as adults went into the building to vote. Meanwhile, officials wearing National-Socialist Party uniforms walked around and gave all children a small flag bearing the swastika. We jumped up and down, waving the flags shouting, "Vote for Adolf Hitler, vote for Adolf Hitler!" For us that was fun.

The SA men (*Sturmabteilung* — they provided protection for Nazi rallies and assemblies) occasionally held meetings in our town, and when they did, they marched down the street by our hotel in their brown uniforms, singing "fatherland" songs. Trudel, Elisabeth, and I watched them pass by from a second story window in the front hallway that contained the inner guest rooms. It was an area where we seldom went. During this time, I also had a job to earn a little pocket money. I pushed baby strollers for working mothers while they helped with their family businesses so that their babies could be out in the fresh air. This also made me wish for a baby sibling, especially for a baby brother. A neighbor lady told me that if I set out a plate of sugar, the stork, who likes that sort of thing, would come for the sugar and bring a baby brother. So, I placed a plate of sugar on the window sill of one of the windows in that second-floor hallway. Then I forgot about it until the SA men marched by again. As my sisters and I ran up to the hallway window, I noticed that the sugar on the plate was gone! I was so excited. I exclaimed to Elisabeth, "The sugar is gone! The stork was here! I'm going to get a baby brother!" She replied, "Oh, I ate that. I wondered why there was sugar on the window sill." I never did get my baby brother.

My sisters and I shared a bedroom. We didn't spend a lot of time together. Since they were two and four years older than me, they had their own friends and they also had to help more in the restaurant and hotel. Because I was still younger, I didn't have to do much. In the evenings, we had to go to bed early. If it was still light enough, we read books, or we just talked. I loved to hear the poems from Goethe or Schiller that my sisters learned in school, and asked them to recite them for me, which they did. By the time I was in their grades, I already knew all the poems by heart. I turned more to Trudel to help me with my school work. Elisabeth was too much of a perfectionist and often became impatient with me. Elisabeth and I did play more together, but also often fought. She had long fingernails and could draw blood when she scratched my skin. She was the first of us girls to use make-up and paint her fingernails; I was too much of a tomboy and was not interested in that type of thing at all.

Although I was healthy then, I was still very thin, probably because I was always very lively. My mother said I was nervous. While I still had my baby teeth, the front teeth had a gap between them and there was an old wives' tale that said that meant I was going to take a long trip sometime in my lifetime. Whenever I smiled at a stranger, they told me that I would travel far someday. My hair was also thin, so my mother kept cutting it. It was straight, chestnut brown, and cut straight across below my ears, framing my broad face. My bangs were short, cut straight across my forehead, high above my hazel eyes, but I longed to have long, thick hair that I could wear in braids like most of the other girls.

Because I was so skinny, my mother tried constantly to overfeed me. I didn't like that she put extra thick layers of butter on my bread or that I had to drink malt beer (no or very little alcohol) containing a raw egg yolk with my supper. Every afternoon we would meet as a family and have coffee time together. My sisters and I drank *Milchkaffee*, coffee that was mostly milk and some sugar. With that we had a *Brötchen*, a hard roll, with marmalade and butter, or, if business went well that day, we could run to the bakery and buy something sweet. On Sundays, we had cake with the coffee. My mother didn't bake much, but sometimes she prepared several sheets of plum cake, or at Christmas time, *Stolle*, and then took them to the baker who baked them for her. The cakes turned out better that way because the baker had special ovens, whereas at home the baking was done in wood-burning ovens, which were unpredictable.

Those Sunday coffee times were opportunities for families to visit each other, but we rarely had anyone from Schmölz come for a visit. They were country people and needed to stay home to tend their livestock and keep the home fires burning. Most people living rurally also still traveled with horse drawn wagons and the distances took much longer than by car. But one Sunday we did get quite a surprise. It was the Sunday before Trudel's confirmation. Confirmation at that time consisted of two Sundays: an examination Sunday, followed by the confirmation Sunday for those who passed their exam. One good thing about this was that you got two new dresses, one for each of those two Sundays. The test was taken orally in front of the congregation as part of the regular service. Boys lined up on a bench on one side in front of the altar and girls lined up on the other side. Various questions were asked of each confirmand and some parts had to be memorized. Trudel flew through her answers with flying colors. After the exam, we went back home and prepared to enjoy a normal Sunday afternoon. We had just finished with the noon meal when we saw a big limousine, driven by a chauffeur, stop in front of the hotel. We curiously walked to the doorway and saw people we didn't recognize at first getting out of the limousine. It was *Tante* Babette (Aunt Babette) and

Onkel Paul (Uncle Paul) and their young son, Hermann. They wanted to come to the confirmation ceremony but had arrived a week early. What a surprise! My mother immediately scurried around to find something to eat for them and then we had a very nice Sunday afternoon visit with them. *Tante* Babette was a sister of my mother, and her husband, *Onkel* Paul, owned a paint and varnish factory in Erfurt. Because of her previous lifestyle, she and my mother were not very close. She had divorced her first husband for this rich, older man. Although she financially took care of her son, Bernhard, from the previous marriage, she had left him to grow up with his father.

The next weekend was the confirmation ceremony. This was a really big event for a young person because at age fourteen, he or she transitioned from being a child to being a grown up. Little boys, for example, wore only short pants with knee socks. After confirmation, they were considered young men and could wear long trousers. My mother, my sisters, and I all had to have new dresses for the occasion. *Fräulein* Glückmann, an elderly seamstress, had come to our house several weeks before to take our measurements. She came a second time for us to try on the semi-finished product before presenting us with the finished dresses. There were no stores where you could go to buy dresses. To get a new dress, you would look through a book, pick out a style you liked, and a tailor or seamstress would make it for you. Elisabeth and I received different styles from the same dark green fabric, but Trudel was required to wear a black dress. A few relatives were able to come for the Sunday celebration, as well as many neighbors. My mother had also invited all of Trudel's teachers and their wives. Sunday afternoon was only one of three afternoons where people came to celebrate and have coffee and cake. This resulted in a large amount of presents, many of which were items for Trudel's hope chest.

Tante Rettel, my father's oldest sister, who was a tiny woman with white hair and a wrinkled face, had come on Saturday to help with preparations for Sunday's big event. As the day went on, she developed a terrible headache that would not go away. My father called the doctor to see if he would prescribe some medication. The doctor replied, "Sure, send someone over and I will give them some pills for your sister". My father suggested *Tante* Rettel take two or three so they would take effect faster, which she did. Soon after, she became very dizzy. A closer look at the label on the pill box revealed my aunt had taken sleeping tablets, not pills for a headache! She slept the rest of the day. When it was time to go to church the next morning, my mother could only wake her long enough to take her to the bathroom before she fell asleep again. She slept through the entire confirmation service and the festivities that followed. My father was very angry with that doctor!

Besides being confirmed at fourteen, you could also be finished with school and begin an apprenticeship unless you were in a higher academic level school and planned to study at a university later. Trudel chose to be finished with school. My father felt she should learn to be a chef for the hotel industry and sent her to begin her apprenticeship with a wealthy acquaintance in Oschersleben. She was very unhappy there because she was nothing more than a maid and felt she wasn't learning a trade.

My parents' business was doing well. The Autobahn had not yet been built so all traffic, including much motorcycle traffic, from Berlin or Magdeburg to the Harz Mountains passed through the city of Gröningen, right past our hotel. Whenever something special was going on in the Harz Mountain area, streams of cars would drive by. When all the overnight accommodations near the mountains were full, the establishments in Gröningen benefited. Sometimes when we were overbooked, my parents would give up their bedroom and sleep on two extra beds in our big bedroom.

A huge motorcycle race took place in Europe at this time that covered several countries, including Germany, and passed though Gröningen. The street had been prepared with high stacks of straw bales at the curve by the hotel so that someone who wiped out would be less likely to hurt themselves or the buildings. The scheduled time to pass through Gröningen was around midnight. People thronged the street to see the cyclists pass by. My father took advantage of this opportunity by staying open all night. He brought all the chairs from inside the restaurant and placed them out along the street. He sold a lot of beer and other beverages that night. When the cyclists drove by, their motors roared loudly and they were covered with dust. We children enjoyed all the excitement and were allowed to stay up and watch most of the race.

That tight curve gave us many hours of entertainment during rainy days. The motorcyclists would often attempt to show off their skills by maneuvering around the curve on wet pavement without slowing down. Many wiped out and that was our entertainment. Fortunately, they wore heavy rain gear and did not hurt themselves.

Running a hotel and restaurant brought a great deal of work, so my mother's youngest sister, Klara, came to work as a maid and stayed three years. She had finished school in Schmölz at the required age of fourteen and wanted an opportunity to get out of that poor area and learn a skill. While in Gröningen, she met Erich Wust, whose wealthy parents owned the meat market next door to our building. They later married. *Herr* Wust was one of the few in town who owned a car. He sometimes took me along for a ride when he ran errands. He liked me and called me nicknames like "Murmann's Zigeuner" (Murmann's gypsy) or "Hans", because of my short hair. He also gave me presents for my birthday. One year he gave me a pretty tea cup and saucer. The tea cup was filled with chocolates with a big bow on top. I was like a granddaughter to him. His son, Erich, went into apprenticeship to become a baker, and when he was finished, his father bought him a building in Dessau, which also contained a bakery.

Directly across the street from our hotel was another hotel, "Zum Deutschen Haus", which was our competition, although many said my mother's cooking was better. She made home-style meals which the truck drivers for the sugar factory especially liked. But Zum Deutchen Haus had added a large hall in which they showed movies every Sunday afternoon. These movies were the silent ones at first with a piano player banging on the keys to provide the music, while subtitles appeared at the bottom of the screen. Two series that I remember were a "Tom Mix" western and "Pat und Patachon," featuring two comical men doing silly things. We girls loved going to the movies, but my parents were very stingy with their money because they were saving up for future opportunities, so most times only Trudel and Elisabeth were given money for the movie, since they were older. As they stood in line to buy their tickets, I would simply walk in. I was just a little kid and no one paid attention to me, so I always got in free.

Holidays were special times, especially Christmas. The four weeks before Christmas were the advent weeks. People made advent wreathes from fresh pine branches. Ours was approximately three feet in diameter and hung from the ceiling in our entryway. It had four red candles and each Sunday before Christmas one more candle was lit until all four were burning. We would light these candles for a short time each evening. Advent calendars also hung on our window. During this time, when we got together with our friends, we were less likely to play games. Rather, we brought yarn or some embroidery along to make Christmas gifts and worked on that together.

December 6 was St. Nikolas Day. Before we went to bed on St. Nikolas Eve, we opened the front window and put our shoes on the windowsill. The next morning, we found candies in our shoes. St. Nikolas didn't come and visit us, but somehow he knew that we had been good. Had we not been good our shoes would have been empty, which never happened for us.

On December 24, we were no longer allowed to enter the meeting room that was off of the big kitchen. The atmosphere was almost secretive. That's where the Christmas tree was being decorated and we weren't allowed to see it. In the early evening my mother, sisters, and I went to church while my father stayed home to let the *Weihnachtsmann* (Santa Claus) in, in case he came by. I was eight years old and still believed in the *Weihnachtsmann* at that point. The restaurant was closed for the evening. When we returned home, we entered the kitchen and my father opened the door to the meeting room. What a wonderful sight awaited us! All the candles on the Christmas tree were lit. The smell of the burning candles and fresh pine wafted out at us while our sights were on the warm, bright glow in the room. My eyes also went to the confections that were hung on the tree along with the bulbs and to the table beside it on which sat a large bowl piled high with oranges, dates, figs, and nuts. Beside that were plates of various Christmas cookies. They all added to the mixture of smells.

That year I had wished for a doll. There, beside the tree, I saw a large doll in a pretty dress with a life-like face and short brown hair. At that time, the hair on dolls was made from real hair that you could brush and comb. Beside it were some books, some small clothing items, and a game. The presents were not wrapped. Each child found her pile of gifts, nicely arranged. In my wishes, I had wanted my doll to have long hair that I could braid. All of my friends had long hair that was braided, but I had very short haircuts because my hair was so thin. My doll was supposed to have long hair so that I would have something to braid. I told my mother this and she replied, "Then I'll just have to have a talk with the *Weihnachtsmann* and maybe next year he can bring long hair for your doll". The next year I found my doll beside the Christmas tree with long beautiful braids! My mother had taken my doll to the toy maker, and I hadn't even noticed that the doll was gone. I was ecstatic!

My sisters, of course, didn't believe in the *Weihnachtsmann* anymore and I could not understand why they acted so silly when I sat down to write my letter to him. The year I was nine years old, it was already the evening of the 23rd of December and my family was sitting in the kitchen when there was a knock on the door. My mother went to the door and exclaimed, "It's the *Weihnachtsmann* at our door!" She opened the door for him and the *Weihnachtsmann*, dressed in his usual red cap, big white beard, small rimmed glasses, belted coat, and black boots, holding a whip and a small bag, entered. I was so afraid of this man, although he looked like he might be nice. (A man from the neighborhood was paid by families to play the *Weihnachtsmann*.) We three girls were asked to line up and he asked us questions about our behavior at school and at home. But my sisters kept giggling, so he playfully whipped them and they ran away. I simply could not understand their behavior! I dutifully stood there and politely answered all his questions. He then gave me a few sweet treats because I had been such a good girl, and he departed.

Easter was another big holiday for me. The day before, we put grass in our Easter baskets to make a little nest in each and set them out for the Easter bunny. After we went to bed, my mother colored the eggs and hid them early on Easter morning in our courtyard. After we hunted the eggs and found candies and a big chocolate Easter bunny in our baskets, we ate some of the eggs for breakfast and then we girls went to the children's service at the church. We always got a new spring dress for Easter. My parents stayed at home because this was a very busy day in the restaurant. There were many travelers who stopped to have their noon meal before their drive to visit others.

When I was nine years old, my sisters both got new bicycles for Easter. I didn't get one because I hadn't learned how to ride a bicycle yet. I was given Elisabeth's old one. That same afternoon, Trudel and Elisabeth tried to help me. On the street behind our hotel we tried time after time. They held on while I tried to pedal, but I always fell when they let go. After a while, they tired of this and went off to visit friends, but I was determined to learn. So, I got back on the bike and tried by myself. To my surprise, it worked. Suddenly I found myself rolling forward and continuing to roll, but when I got far enough away, I realized that I didn't know how to stop. I knew you had to push back on the pedals, so I did this but with so much force that the bike jolted, and I fell forward on my face. I really hadn't hurt myself badly, so I got back on that bike and rode it home. Everyone was surprised at how quickly I had taught myself to ride a bicycle.

❦

Because there was not much traffic on the *Grabenstraße*, I was not careful to look for traffic, and one day I stepped out in front of a moped. A farmer, who was an acquaintance, was driving. We saw each other, but I misjudged and thought I could beat him. He hit the leg with which I had already stepped off the curb, and I immediately fell and hit my head on the pavement. The maid for the Wust family was shaking out rugs and saw what happened. She immediately ran over to me and called for my mother, who came out of the hotel crying. She thought I was dead because I had lost consciousness. You could also see where the tire had torn the skin all the way on my leg. They carried me to one of the guest rooms in the hotel and called the doctor, who came immediately. He brought along all his supplies so he could anesthetize me, and he stitched up all the wounds up my leg. I was delirious for the next three days, but when I felt better, I had many visitors and was spoiled by my family. The farmer and his wife came to visit every day. Even though my leg was elevated for several weeks, I spent my time visiting with people, reading, and doing schoolwork. When I was finally able to return to school, my leg was thickly wrapped because the wounds were still seeping a little, and I had to hobble along on crutches. I didn't want to go because I knew the boys would make fun of me, and they did.

Every year there was a *Schützenfest* in Gröningen that lasted several days. A *Schützenfest* is a "marksmen's festival". It is a traditional festival found in many German cities and features a target shooting competition for men, target competitions for the youth, a parade, and a fair with rides, food, and drink. On the first afternoon, children participated in a parade for which the girls wore a wreath of flowers on their heads. We first had to walk to the local flower shop to get these. The boys carried a hollow staff with a small bouquet of flowers sticking out of the top. We paraded through the town with a small band playing in front of us followed by the members of the *Schützenverein* (the marksmen's club), *das Luisenbund* (the women's club), and us children. Then we proceeded to a large meadow outside of town that had booths set up, carousels, and a large tent for dancing later in the evening. Beyond that was an area set up for our competitions. The girls had to try to throw a ball through a wreath of flowers. The girl who could accomplish this three times had the chance to become *Schützenprinzessin* (princess). The boys blew darts from a pipe to a cardboard target. The winner became the prince. I participated, of course, but in the six years we lived there, I could not throw the ball through the wreath three times. My friend, Margaret Gröber, though, was successful and she became the *Schützenprinzessin*. The men also had a building there where they had their competitions, from which the *Schützenkönig* (king) was then chosen. After the competitions, we enjoyed the rides, the food, and being with our friends. My parents gave us a small amount of money for these afternoons. When I was hungry I could have bought a bratwurst, a *Herringsbrötchen* (fish sandwich), cakes, cookies, or so many other things, but I usually spent all my money on licorice. I loved licorice! One time I ran out of money before the afternoon was over. I walked back home, pestered my mother until she gave in and gave me more money. She had a little tin with pennies in it that she said I could have. I put them all in my handkerchief and raced back to the meadow.

The next morning, a band marched to Margaret's house and picked her up, as they had done for the prince and the king. I was so happy for her. She looked very pretty in a new, white dress and a wreath of flowers ringing her blonde hair. She, the prince, and the king rode on a platform in another parade to the meadow for more festivities. It was great fun!

The next year, after the new princess had been chosen, the Gröbers were required to host the new princess, her family, and others in the parade with a luncheon and cake and coffee. They had many tables set out in their yard, with one table containing all the food. When someone accepted the "princess" position, the family had to plan to do this the following year. If a girl successfully threw three times through the flowered hoop, she could always decline if she thought her family could not afford to do this, but Margaret was an only child and the Gröbers were proud of her.

⚬≈⚬

In 1935, Gröningen had a huge 1,000 year celebration. Dignitaries, reporters, and tourists came from all over Germany. My mother had hired the seamstress to make new dresses for this occasion, and we also bought new shoes. My new shoes were a beige patent leather and very pretty. Our guest rooms were filled with reporters, and of course they took their meals in our restaurant. Some befriended us girls and took pictures of us. Part of the celebration included a parade where all participants were elaborately dressed and coaches were presented as they had looked 1,000 years ago. The former arched gates with side towers of the medieval Gröningen had been replicated from structures made from cardboard and wood to look exactly as they had those many years ago. The celebrations with carousels and tents for games, eating, and dancing took place in a meadow on the outskirts of the town. My father rented two large tents. All of our relatives and various friends from near and far came to help transport food, pour beer, wait on tables, or clear off the tables in the tents. Erich Wust helped out a lot because he was already courting Klärchen, as we called my *Tante* Klara. The children's job was to pull a wagon back and forth from the restaurant with items that had been forgotten, but needed. When the wagon was empty, I rode in the wagon. During one trip, instead of sitting, I knelt and when I got out, I was shocked to see that I had totally scuffed the toes of my brand new shoes. You can be sure I heard about that later!

The next bigger city to Gröningen was Halberstadt, and at times my mother rode the bus there to do some shopping. That's where we bought our shoes. But shopping was still limited in Halberstadt. The closest big city with many wonderful stores was Magdeburg. One summer day in 1935, a business acquaintance of my father offered to take my mother in the side seat of his motorcycle to Magdeburg to shop. She took me along, and I sat on her lap. What an experience of a lifetime that was for me, to go speeding along the highway, rushing through the wind, the loud motor droning in our ears! We had a windshield in front of us and wore headscarves, so the trip was very comfortable and we arrived in one piece.

When I was ten, I was able to join the Hitler Youth. You had to be ten years old to join, and I was excited because it was a fairly new organization in our town. At this time, it was not mandatory to be in the Hitler Youth, but I couldn't wait to join. The meetings took place in a large empty room of a business building. During the meetings, we learned and sang a variety of songs and played a variety of games including charades, but there was also a lecture time where we learned about history and other facts about the National Socialistic Party and about Adolf Hitler. We also practiced how to march together, keeping in proper step. Many of the songs we learned lent themselves well to singing while we were marching, so we always sang to keep in step. When the weather was nice, our small group marched to the open meadow outside of town where we played ball games and had relay races. The meetings lasted approximately one to two hours and took place once a week in the afternoon. I enjoyed the companionship of my friends and thought the meetings were a lot of fun.

3

TEENAGE YEARS
MAGDEBURG, 1936-1943

For the average German, these years began with contentment. Life was good, but not for the Jewish people. Hitler had control of the newspapers and radio, where he promoted his propaganda against the Jews. Some believed the propaganda of Jewish "relocation," some didn't, and most young people did not concern themselves either way. Nevertheless, young people's lives were changed. The Hitler Youth for boys put more emphasis on pre-military training, and at age eighteen they were inducted in the Reichsarbeitsdienst (RAD — Reich work service) for six months, followed by three years of military service unless they were studying at a university. Girls were also strongly encouraged to join the Jungmädel or the BDM (Bund Deutsher Mädel), both auxiliaries of the Hitler Youth, and they were also obligated to work in the RAD for six months when they turned eighteen.

Germans were also told by Hitler that the country needed to expand to the East to be able to feed its people. When war with Poland broke out in September 1939, the ordinary public was depressed, even horrified to be involved in war again, and they

hoped it would be short and that all would be back to normal.
But in May 1940, the German Blitzkrieg (lightning war) was
launched against Holland, Belgium, Luxembourg, and France.
In August, the air offensive against Britain began, and by 1941,
the air war was raging over Germany with alarms and raids
every other night. Food, clothing, gasoline, and household items
were rationed. Coal to heat homes was growing scarce. In June
1941, Hitler invaded Russia, and on December 11, 1941, he
declared war on the United States, and the German people knew
their plight would not be over soon.

ᘗᕬᕟᕬᘖ

Although my parents were doing well financially, further
success was limited at the Gröningen location. So in 1936,
my father went to Magdeburg, (a city of approximately
300,000 people) to scout for another possibility. He found
a restaurant in the northern part of the city that was part
of a six-story building on the corner of Königsstraße and
Rudolfsstraße and was owned by the Schultheis Brewery.
The restaurant had been owned by an elderly couple
who could no longer care for it properly. The run-down
appearance and loss of clientele made the property more
affordable. My father was able to buy the restaurant
including all the inventory within.

When it came time to move, all of our furniture and
other belongings were packed into a moving truck. Large
suitcases, which we were taking ourselves, contained our
clothing and were set by the front door. After the truck
departed, my parents, Elisabeth, and I (Trudel was still in
Oschersleben, training) were picked up by an acquaintance
and driven to the railway station. From there we took the
train to Bad Nauheim to vacation a few weeks with my

uncle and aunt, Adam and Leni Scheler. It was the first time that my father and mother were able to take a vacation together with us, and that made me so happy.

The time we spent there was relaxing and enjoyable. Since Bad Nauheim is a spa city, my mother took advantage of the baths and spa treatments and my father relaxed in the back yard with a good book. The house was actually a *Pension* (similar to a bed and breakfast, except you could get two or three meals and often people stayed several days to a week). My *Tante* Leni operated the *Pension*. The basement contained a large kitchen with a broad window that faced a beautiful yard. The main floor had a large dining area for the guests, and the upper floors contained the guests' rooms. *Tante* Leni let me help her in various ways in the kitchen and I really enjoyed that, especially when it came time to lick the dessert bowls.

After two weeks, my parents drove on to Magdeburg to open the new restaurant and to meet the moving truck with the furniture. Elizabeth and I stayed two weeks longer. The time went by quickly. Elisabeth and I walked somewhere every morning. Some of our favorite places were the tennis courts where we watched people hit the ball back and forth, a large pond where we fed the swans and ducks stale bread pieces, and a luxury hotel in the center of Bad Nauheim. We sat on a bench across from the hotel and watched as big limousines pulled up to the front door. A Moor, a short statured black man with a turban around his head, would jump from the back of the limousine and grab all the suitcases or hold an umbrella for those getting out while other employees from the hotel lined up to help the elegantly dressed guests. It seemed as though we were watching a movie unfold in front of us. One evening we watched my very first fireworks that took place over the pond. I was amazed at the brilliant colors, the falling stars, and the combination of various lights as they danced in the sky. One thing Elisabeth and I were not allowed to do in their home was to sing Hitler Youth songs. Sometimes, without thinking, we would begin to sing them and our aunt would say, "Those aren't allowed in our house!" *Onkel* Adam and *Tante* Leni were actually communists.

The Olympics were taking place at this time in Berlin, and when it came time for us to take the train to Magdeburg, my aunt arranged for us to be accompanied by her friend, who was also taking that train to Berlin to watch the Olympic games. We got off the train in Magdeburg and expected to see one of our parents there to meet us because my aunt had sent them a card with our arrival time. We stood on the platform with our heavy suitcases and did not see anyone that we knew. We waited and waited but no one came. Elisabeth said that maybe they didn't get the card in time, but we could not call them or even take the streetcar to Königsstraße because, although our aunt had packed some sandwiches for us, she had not given us any money. Elisabeth finally suggested that we walk to our *Onkel* Otto's bar that was only a few blocks from the train station, so we lugged our heavy suitcases a short way, stopped to rest, lugged some more, stopped to rest, and continued this pattern until we reached *Onkel* Otto's bar. The bar didn't open until 5:00, so when we arrived there no one was around. Elisabeth suggested that I stay with the suitcases and she would walk the long way to the new restaurant, asking for directions as she went. She was gone a

long time. While I waited, I noticed older children playing
in the narrow street. I felt strange in this big city and was
becoming scared. Suddenly I saw my father walking toward
me. "You poor *Mäuschen* (little mouse)! We received no
card telling us you were coming!" he exclaimed. (It arrived
the next day.) He took the suitcases, and we walked to and
boarded the streetcar and rode to my new home.

ᘒᘏ

It was exciting to see the newly renovated restaurant. The
address was Königstraße 13. The view of the front of the
grey, stucco building was of a large, arched entryway with
five broad, stone steps leading up to a shallow landing at the
front door. My father's name was etched in large letters above
the arch. A tall tree shaded two terraces on either side of
the entryway. The terraces were filled with several tables and
chairs, and ivy grew on trellises, forming a wall around them.
My friends would later comment that I had it so nice: I could
eat all the good restaurant food and do my homework sitting
out on a terrace. To the right, beyond the terrace, another
arched double doorway led to the courtyard within.

When you stepped through the front door into a
vestibule and turned right, you were in the *Jägerszimmer*, a
room where the hunters' club and other organizations met.
One wall was filled with hunting trophies (most were deer
and wild boar), and there were several alcoves. Dark ebony
wainscot covered the lower half of the walls, which gave
the room a cozy appearance. Facing the Königsstraße in
the front were two large windows that brightened the room
during the daytime. As you entered the restaurant to the
left, you couldn't help but notice the large bay windows that
faced both the Königsstraße and the Rudolfstraße, which

crossed at a forty-five degree angle. Next to the last bay window were two smaller, stained glass windows under which was the large, round *Stammtisch*, a table permanently reserved for family and friends. In the evenings, friends gathered around this table, had friendly conversations, and enjoyed their beer. From here a few steps led to a door that opened into another gathering room. In this room were a coin operated French billiard table (using three balls), pin ball machines, and a piano, as well as more tables. The machines and billiard table were owned by a company that sent a representative once a week to collect the coins. I learned that if I stuck around when they came, they would give me a small tip for helping them sort the coins. Another door led to the toilets and to an entrance to the Rudolfstraße where our residence was located. There were also two large rooms on the second floor where groups could meet privately and be served meals. Above that were four more stories containing apartments. The apartments whose entry door faced the Königsstraße were inhabited by wealthy families. They were bigger and had balconies, hot and cold running water, and full bathrooms. Those who lived there with their families were of various professions: a doctor, a dentist, a professor, a businessman, an auditor, an artist, a bank director, and a record salesman. The apartments on the side of the Rudolfstraße were also very nice and had running water (cold only), but had only a toilet and a sink — no shower or bathtub. The custodian of the building and our housemaids lived in rooms on the uppermost floor.

The door to our private residence faced the Rudolfsstraße, A small entryway separated an inner door and outer door, and, off to the side, a narrow stairway led to the upper floor apartments. Beyond the inner door was a hallway. The first door on the left in the hallway led to a guest room. This room had a big mirror where we girls often fixed our hair. The next room on the right contained a toilet and a sink. Then came our bedroom. It was a long room with a big window that looked out into our courtyard. In that room we had three beds, a large wardrobe cabinet, and a dresser with a mirror. We each had one drawer for ourselves. Each of us also had a nightstand by our bed and a chair. In one corner was a *Kachelofen* (a stove made from special tiles) that was only heated in the coldest weather or if one of us was sick in bed. At the end of the hallway you entered the large living/dining room combination. It contained a couch, a dining table with four brown, leather-backed chairs, a large wood credenza, a bookcase, a *Kachelofen*, and a cabinet containing a record player and radio. My father hooked up extra speakers in the restaurant so our customers could enjoy the music as well. On the credenza set a Delft vase and two silver candelabras, each candelabra having five low arms that curved upward at the ends and each held a candle. The room contained two other doors: one to my parents' bedroom and one to the restaurant kitchen. Each room had an area rug on the wooden floor and the hallway had a runner. We periodically had to roll up the rugs, take them outside, hang them over the clothesline, and beat the dust out of them.

Though the restaurant had central heating from a large furnace located in the basement, our residence was heated only by the *Kachelofen* in each room. Because we didn't spend a lot of time there, the stoves weren't heated on a regular basis, and our apartment was often cold. In the winter, before we went to bed, we heated ceramic bottles of water in the kitchen oven and took them to bed with us. We laid them under the feather beds, which were our covers; first near the headboard and then, when we were ready to crawl under into bed, we rolled them down to the foot. They stayed warm for quite a long time. There were times when the room was so cold that the water in the bottles, which had rolled from the bed during the night, had frozen! Getting up then was torture and we only had cold water at the sink. Because our apartment faced the Rudolfstraße, our residence, like the other apartments on that side, only had the sink and toilet.

Magdeburg was a very pretty, walled-in, medieval city located on the Elbe River. It did have industry, but most of the industries that polluted the air were located further north, beyond the city. Magdeburg had many nice residential areas, many parks, and a beautiful, famous cathedral with a large open area in front of it. The cathedral contained many valuable works of art and statues. The city and the cathedral had been damaged and rebuilt several times throughout its turbulent history. There were also two theaters, *das Zentraltheater* (the central theater) and *das Stadttheater* (the city theater). The central theater was not far from our restaurant and often children's performances took place there. Whenever a new play or ballet took place, I was allowed to go to these wonderful, live performances. There were also many movie theaters, which my friends and I enjoyed.

After a few days of getting settled in, my father took us to our new school, *Diesterwegschule*, a girls' school which was a thirty minute walk from our home. It was a middle school that only went to age sixteen. I met my teacher, *Fräulein* Müller. She was in her 50's, thin, with wire-rimmed glasses, her wavy gray hair pulled back in a bun. Her dress hung loosely, not stylish at all. Throughout the time I had her as a teacher, she wore that kind of dress or straight, long skirts and blouses. She was very strict but very nice. She treated everyone fairly and gave praise when it was deserved. When someone forgot their breakfast sandwich, which we ate at break time, she shared her own and said, "Shared joy is double joy". This only happened to me once. She was not married, but teaching was her passion, and she found joy in doing special things for her students. When we arrived at school the day before Christmas break we were forbidden to go into the classroom. We hung our coats on the hooks in the hallway and waited. When we were allowed to enter, we saw a lit candle on each of our desks with a small green wreath, an apple, and a few cookies. If someone had a birthday, he found a wreath of flowers and a lit candle on his desk and could choose the song to start the day. We began each day singing a hymn and reciting a prayer. Later in 1940, I had to drop out of school because my father was drafted into the army and my mother needed my help to run the restaurant. On my very last day *Fräulein* Müller asked me to stand up. Then she gave a speech to the class, praising me and my accomplishments and saying how much she was going to miss me. Later in life, I learned that *Fräulein* Müller had been a school friend of my mother-in-law!

Fräulein Müller taught English and German. She was also our class teacher and in charge of our classroom, where we stayed for the entire school day unless we had art or gym. When another teacher came into our classroom to teach their subject, we immediately stood up and greeted him or her. Then they told us to be seated and we sat down. The teacher of the other classroom for my age group was also the French teacher and we went to her classroom when it was time for French class, so the French class was a combination of girls from both her classes and *Fräulein* Müller's class. It was still a very small class for two reasons. You had to have an excellent grade, a 1 (equal to the American A), before you could take a second language, and also no one liked her, so many opted out. She always favored the girls from her own classroom, which of course made us angry. With so few in the class, she was able to keep a close eye on all of us. She was skinny, ugly, and mean spirited. She took pride in the fact that she had lived in France and could speak excellent French, but she over-pronounced her French to the point that it was comical and she spoke in a very sing-songy voice. That caused us girls to giggle and, naturally when we looked at each other we often could not hold it in.

Our history teacher was also a character and very strict. He freely gave *Backpfeifen*, slaps on the face, not just for bad behavior but also if you didn't have your work done. He expected us to be model students, but there were some in the class who couldn't sit still, who talked too much, or who were lazy. One day he had had it with us. He stormed out of the room and shortly came back with Elisabeth. He made her stand in front of the class and proceeded to lecture us on how we should be more like her: hard working, all work always completed, all grades excellent, etc. Poor Elisabeth didn't even know what was going on. She was a model student and deserved much praise but not in this fashion. Whenever someone had a birthday, he asked them to come forward and gave them a *Pfennig* (penny). He said, "Put this into your pocket because it is a lucky penny." He did the same for all students, never changing his routine.

I liked my new school. Behind our school was a large open area where we spent our fifteen-minute breaks. Beyond that was a big building and that was the boys' school. The girls were always dismissed before the boys so that we were gone by the time their school let out. So, we had no contact with them. It was also strongly forbidden to look out of the windows when the boys had their recess!

One day one of our classmates, who had had an appendicitis operation and had been absent for several weeks, returned for a brief visit with her dog. They were below our classroom window in the open courtyard. We had just returned to the classroom from recess and the history teacher wasn't in the room yet. She wanted to show us some of the tricks that her dog could do, so without thinking twice about it, the whole class stood at the window and watched the tricks being performed below. Suddenly the teacher came into the room, but he made us all line up in the front and gave us each a slap in the face! The slap burned a little, but we all thought it was funny, and it was difficult to hold in our giggles!

We took all the basic subjects each year: German, history, math, sciences, geography, English, French, literature, music, religion, art, physical education, and *Handarbeit* (needle work). I found geography interesting and liked learning about other countries. All the maps were kept in a storeroom and when it came time to study a certain part of the world, one of us was given the task of getting the map from the storeroom. When it was my turn, I was amazed at all the maps and globes stored in that little room. For art class, we went to the uppermost floor of the building. There were sky windows in the roof for optimal lighting. This was my favorite subject. We worked with many different forms of art. In the *Handarbeitsklasse*, we learned more advanced ways to knit, crochet, darn socks, mend clothes, and sew. Four times a week we had Sport (physical education) and we were told, "In a healthy body grows a healthy spirit". We played games such as *Schlagball* (similar to baseball), where you had to hit a small ball with a bat. Then you had to run to a point (goal) while the player who caught the ball tried to throw it at you and hit you with it. Aiming for the head was not allowed! If they missed and you reached your goal, you scored a point for your team. If you were hit, you were out. I also enjoyed *Völkerball* (dodgeball). When we did gymnastics on bars, ropes, rings, or on mats, I was always picked to demonstrate. I must have had the most athletic ability in my class. I also loved music class. I loved to sing and had a pleasant, high soprano voice. We always sang with three or four voices, harmonizing each song. My least favorite subject was German. We were required to write a lot as perfectly and neatly as possible and to use good grammar. Math came easily for me. I liked practicing the various tables, especially multiplication and division, and was able to easily memorize them. When our math teacher entered the room, he had us sit down with a unique method. He called out someone's name and a quick math problem and in order to be able to sit down, we had to immediately repeat the problem with the correct answer. I was always able to sit right away.

The highlight of the school year was a trip to the Harz Mountains. *Fräulein* Müller, along with the physical education teacher, took us for a week each year. They arranged for us, along with several parents who served as chaperones, to stay in a youth hostel. We slept on the second floor in a big room filled with approximately ten bunkbeds. The chaperones cooked simple meals for us in the hostel's kitchen, and we ate our evening meals at long, wooden tables with benches. In the mornings, we ate *Müsli* (a wholesome mixture of various grains, fruits, and/or nuts) for our breakfast while the chaperones prepared sandwiches to take along on our daily hikes. We would hike most of the day, but we also had breaks in which we sat on the ground and listened to short lectures or readings, sang, played guessing games, or ate our sandwiches. During one of these rest periods, my good friend, Elisabeth Holste, sang a song, a familiar tune in which she had created new verses. Each verse described a student in our class. We then joined in singing the refrain, eager to hear the next verse. In the evenings, we were allowed to relax or practice skits which were presented on the last evening of our stay.

Several nights before bedtime, as we sat on our beds, we played evening songs on our wooden flutes. We had all been trained in school to play them. Some played large alto flutes and the rest played the normal soprano flutes. *Fräulein* Müller loved to hear us harmonize and it was a beautiful way to end a fun day.

One late afternoon, a bus pulled up filled with school boys. They slept on the main floor. When we began playing our flutes that night, we suddenly heard coughs and the loud clearing of throats below us. That brought us to giggling and we couldn't play on. *Fräulein* Müller called, "Pull yourselves together and keep playing!" So we began again, but soon the coughing started as well. Try as we might, we could not continue, and *Fräulein* Müller finally told us to stop.

At the end of the school year, before the summer vacation began, the schools had a little festival at the baron's estate. Parents were invited to attend this event. Each student brought along an item to be used as a prize for a drawing and the school also furnished larger prizes. Long tables covered with the prizes were set up in one of the estate rooms. You could buy either blue or pink tickets, as many as you wanted. After all the tickets were purchased, an announcement was made whether only blue tickets were eligible to win prizes or the pink ones. So, if you had the wrong color, you didn't have a chance to have your ticket drawn. One year, the night before this school festival, I dreamed that the winning ticket color was blue, so the next day I told several of my friends what I had dreamt and that I was only going to buy blue tickets. Several believed me and bought only blue tickets, and so did I. And sure enough, the color was blue!

One year, when I was twelve years old, my father came to this festival, and that was so special for me because he rarely came to any of my school activities or performances. Several choirs sang and then the classes competed in some sporting events. My class competed in dodgeball, and we lost. I was so angry because my father finally came to see me play, and my team had lost.

Elisabeth and I resumed taking piano lessons. Our teacher was state certified, which meant he was supposed to be very good, but I couldn't stand him and did not like going to him. First of all, he had hay fever and sneezed and snorted constantly. He also made us practice writing musical notes, which I had no interest in doing, and he used a metronome while we were playing. I found the constant ticking very stressful. To get to his place I had to walk pretty far because my father was a penny-pincher and would not give me streetcar money. But one rainy day, my father relented and gave me the money for the streetcar. The directions and streetcar changes that I had to make were somewhat complicated, and I climbed into the wrong streetcar to go to my piano lessons. I rode it in the opposite direction, clear to the end station. I didn't know what to do, so I just sat there and cried. The driver took pity on me and let me ride back for free, but I got to my piano lesson a half hour late. I cried again because I thought the teacher was going to yell at me for letting him wait so long. He didn't. I still quit taking lessons from him a short time later.

Elisabeth and I generally went to bed early because we were still in school. One night, as I was sleeping, she shook me awake and said, "Leni, it's getting light out. The maids forgot to wake us!" It was difficult for me to wake out of my sleepy state, but we both splashed cold water on our faces and quickly dressed for school. As we approached the kitchen to eat a quick breakfast, we noticed the smell of cooked food, and we also heard mumbled sounds coming from the restaurant. Something seemed strange and out of place.

When we opened the kitchen door, there stood my mother making sandwiches for the customers still in the bar area. Her eyes got real big, and she asked, "What are you girls doing up? It's 12:30 a.m."

Elisabeth replied, "I thought it was time to go to school!" She took my hand and led me back to the bedroom.

Again, I joined the local Hitler Youth. Ages ten through fourteen were in the *Jungmädel* group, and those over age fourteen belonged to the BDM (*Bund Deutscher Mädel*). There were various levels of leadership roles that could be attained, and many of us had the desire to achieve the higher levels. We were divided into "sections" of ten to fifteen girls. Four sections comprised a "group". You could become a section leader or even a group leader. I was eventually chosen to be a group leader. We wore uniforms of white blouses with black neckerchiefs that were knotted in the front and held together with a leather ring, dark blue skirts that were buttoned onto the blouses (the older girls wore regular skirts with belts), and brown jackets with the symbol of the Hitler Youth and the swastika on the arm. The symbol of the *Jungmädel* was stitched on the breast pocket of our blouses. If you were a section leader, you also wore an additional black/white cord with your neckerchief. Group leaders wore a green cord. We met on Wednesday evenings and on Saturday afternoons in one of the school's classrooms. We learned songs and were taught about national socialism and about the *Führer*.

During the colder months, when we were inside more, we sewed flannel baby blankets and diapers and crocheted baby items for the *Winterhilfe* (a charity to help the poor during winter time). We had fun doing this. We also participated in a fund raiser where we went into stores to collect money that had been placed in jars by the cash registers. The public could buy whittled items from Bavaria for the *Winterhilfe*, and the money then went to buy necessary items for the poor.

During the warmer months, we had *Ausmarsch* every Saturday morning where our groups took walks into the countryside and then played games. On special occasions, like May Day or Hitler's birthday, all of the many groups marched from their areas of the city into the *Domplatz* (the large open area in front of the cathedral) to listen to speeches. It was quite impressive to see so many gathered in one place. We also performed folk dances where we danced around a big bonfire. A choir provided the music. We wore long, white dresses with short, puffy sleeves, gathered skirts, and colorful sashes tied around our waists. The atmosphere was very festive even though there was also a political air about it.

One time, our group had just come back from camp and a high-level member of the Spanish royalty was visiting the grounds where we had assembled. We were told that we could get her autograph. I immediately ran to her, handed her my pen, and was the first to get a signature. But because she was now using my special pen which opened and closed by turning it and I didn't want it to get misplaced, I stayed right by her side until all others had gotten their autographs. The next day she was pictured in a major newspaper, and guess who was also in the picture, standing right beside her!

One of my jobs as a group leader was to take attendance of the girls that were in my group and also to keep track of who paid the thirty-five *Pfennig* dues for that month. At the end of the month, I had to go to the homes of those who did not pay or show up at the meetings. Was that ever an eye opener for me! The northern part of Magdeburg, where my family and all my friends lived, was mainly a neat and clean residential area. I naively thought that everyone lived like this. However, when I went to some of the addresses that were further away from our northern district and nearer to the big industrial area, I saw the dirty, squalid conditions that some people lived in. When I politely approached the parents with my questions, I was taken aback with their course, rude replies.

When I finished school at age fifteen, I gave up my group leader duties, but I was told that I had to attend the meetings of the BDM, the Hitler Youth organization for girls sixteen years and older. I never went and never joined. By that time, I had lost interest, and my help was needed in the restaurant. I was never reprimanded by anyone for not attending.

The operation of the restaurant ran smoothly. In Gröningen my mother did all the home-style cooking, something she felt comfortable doing. When there were fewer guests, she could take care of them herself. But now a more extensive menu was needed for the increased number of guests. So a cook was hired, as well as two housemaids who cleaned and washed dishes. The restaurant also had an Ober (head waiter), and after he took orders from a table, he took his order slip and gave it to whomever was working behind the bar. The large, dark wooden bar was situated across the back corner of the main room, forming a triangle. Here all the beverages were poured. The order slip was then handed back through a large opening in the door in the back wall which led to the kitchen. When the food was ready the whole process was reversed. At the end of the day, the *Ober* added up his receipts and paid my parents the amount owed for the meals. This is the way it was done in German restaurants. The *Ober* purchased the meals from the restaurant and pretty much resold it to the guests. The tip was already included in the price of the meal, but guests sometimes rounded up to an even number and told the *Ober* to "keep the change" called *Trinkgeld* (a little extra money with which to buy himself a drink). My father had to eventually fire our first *Ober*. He was a middle-aged man and knew his trade but gave in to drinking too much and sometimes didn't show up for work. Then we girls had to step in and do our best until another could be hired.

After the mid-day mealtime was over, my parents had a short break before the lighter evening meal of mostly sandwiches began. Most nights they worked until 1:00 or 2:00 a.m. to accommodate the many guests who just came in for a drink or a light late-night snack. At closing, the waiter removed all the white table cloths and ashtrays from the tables and placed the chairs on the tables. The maids, when they came in early the next morning, could then immediately start to clean the brown linoleum floors. One swept the floors clean, and the other went over them with an electric buffer until they shone like new. After that, they dusted everything in the rooms, replaced the tablecloths, and cleaned ashtrays. This all had to be done by around 8:30 a.m. when people would begin to stop in for a cup of coffee.

One of the maids was my cousin, Lotte, the daughter of my mother's sister, Marie, from Kronach, a small city not far from Schmölz. She was a very good piano player and had a beautiful alto singing voice and could easily harmonize. The other maid had a beautiful soprano voice. Together these two would sing while they were washing dishes or cleaning the kitchen. Sometimes, my mother would have to tell them not to sing too loudly because they could be heard in the restaurant. At times, guests would inquire as to where the beautiful singing was coming from. When they helped us with the cleaning of the large baskets of vegetables, we would all sing together and the time would pass quickly.

Business was heaviest for the Sunday noon meal but also brisk throughout the week. A new government building for workers had been built across the street from the restaurant, and many ate their noon meal with us. The specialty, which drew a lot of business, was the *Thüringer Klöße*, dumplings made from raw, grated potatoes, then cooked and served with pork and gravy or Sauerbraten and gravy.

Since my sisters and I were now older, we were required to help out whenever possible. Trudel and Elisabeth helped with pouring beverages behind the bar and also did some waitressing. One of my regular jobs was to gather newspapers, cut the paper into squares, and bore small holes into them. These were then hung on a little nail in bundles in our toilets for wiping. The newspaper print at that time did not rub off as in later years. Laundry day also required several hours of our time. The tables in the restaurant were covered with white tablecloths, and, together with the cloth napkins and towels, they created a lot of laundry. Once a week, the linens were washed in an over-sized wash machine (a big improvement over boiling them in large kettles, the method used in Gröningen) and hung out to dry on the lines that crisscrossed our courtyard, all year round. There were no dryers. It was too much for us to iron, so when the linens were dry, my sisters, Lotte, and I took the laundry to a *Heißmangel*. These business establishments were located throughout the city and one could take laundry to be ironed by big machines with heated steam rollers. They had various sizes of rollers and we used the big ones. Two of us fed the pieces of laundry through the rollers and two caught the perfectly ironed pieces as they came out the other side. It took several hours to finish the entire load of linens, but we passed the time talking or singing, and it didn't seem like a bad job.

In the spring, summer, and fall each Wednesday and Saturday were market days. My father went to the big marketplace in front of the *Rathaus*, the city building, where the farmers had their fresh fruit and vegetable booths set up. He bought large baskets of produce for the restaurant, and then we spent those afternoons in our courtyard behind the kitchen snapping the ends off of green beans, shelling peas, cleaning strawberries, and other tasks.

Beer delivery was also one of our jobs. People ordered beer from my father, so my sisters and I delivered the two, three, or four-liter dark green glass jugs in a wagon. They gave us a small tip for this. When my father noticed that he was low on beer jugs, we went off again to the various customers and collected the empty jugs. Some became such regular customers that, although I only knew them through this delivery, they gave me nice presents when I later married. We also ran various errands for my mother. My sisters always rode their bicycles to do this, but I walked or ran. Everyone knew me by the skip in my walk or that I was otherwise hopping or running. That's why I was such a skinny child.

Then roller skates became the rage, and we all had them. After I was finished with my homework, I would join my friends to roller skate in the park across from the restaurant, near the new, circular government workers' building. We flew along the paved walkways and swung in a circle as we grabbed onto a light pole in the center of the park. Of course, we also enjoyed riding our bikes together over the bridges of the Elbe River, through some open areas, or onto an old estate of a baron who no longer lived there.

As in Gröningen, I made many friends. One of my classmates, Elisabeth Holste, had a talent for poetry. She could easily compose poems and was able to recite all kinds of poetry by heart, even very long ones, like Goethe's *Die Glocke*. At school, she seemed a little odd and didn't have any friends. We weren't close either until we had to work on a project together, making a first aid kit from cigar boxes. To do this, I went to her home which was in a corner building in the *Altstadt*, the old part of the city where the streets were very narrow and buildings were ancient. Her father had a meat market where only horse meat was sold. As we worked on the kit, making compartments in the boxes, covering it with a sturdy, white paper and painting a red cross on the front, then filling all the compartments with necessary first aid items, I realized that she was a very nice girl, and we became friends.

A friend whom I met in the Hitler youth, Tamara, was born in Russia. Her parents were German. Her father was an engineer for a German company that had been located in Russia. In 1938, he was transferred for a year to Poland. There they lived in a small city that was mostly settled by Germans. Tamara told us stories of how badly Germans in her town were treated by the Polish people. The German children there attended German schools, but one day the schools were suddenly all closed down, and the Germans were told that they had to attend the Polish schools, and it was forbidden to speak German in public. After dark, bands of Polish men and boys passed through the residential streets and threw rocks at the German homes. They closed their wooden shutters so that their windows couldn't be broken, and as they sat inside their homes, they had to listen to the thumping of rocks hitting the sides of their houses. She was so scared that she never went outside on the street by herself after that. She did not understand why this was happening. There just seemed to be a general hatred of Germans by the Polish people. They wanted to drive the Germans out of their country. A classmate, Inge Schwarz, had also moved from Poland and told of the same kind of experiences.

Another friend with whom I became acquainted through the Hitler Youth was named Helga, a pretty girl with long, dark blonde braids. She lived on the third story of a large, beautiful apartment house that was located in the wealthy part of the city, overlooking the Hindenburg Bridge over the Elbe River and an adjoining park. One hot summer day after we had practiced marching, she invited me to come home with her for some lemonade and to play some games. Our lemonade was served by a maid. We laughed and talked while playing board games, and after that, I visited frequently. She liked to play tennis and wanted me to also play. I desperately wanted to, but it required that I join the tennis club, and my parents would not agree to pay for that. Having both come from a background where you worked hard all day to make ends meet or to better yourself, they did not believe in such frivolous things like joining a tennis club. In the winter, the tennis courts were converted into ice skating rinks, so I did get to enjoy doing that with her.

Though I had quite a few friends, I wasn't able to get together with them nearly as often as I had with my friends in Gröningen. Besides working more for my parents, I had much more homework that needed to be done, and by the time we were home and finished with our noon meal, it was 2:00 pm. I also had piano lessons and had to practice the piano every day. Furthermore, many classmates lived a greater distance away than before, and I didn't have the money for the streetcar. Much of any free time I had was taken up by having to walk or ride my bike as transportation. Only when it rained, did I get money for the streetcar. I also didn't play much with boys. They had their own school, and I was simply occupied with work and my own friends.

The Wenzels were another special couple in our lives who lived in Magdeburg. They ran the bakery at the other end of our block. Our block was in the shape of a triangle: the Königsstraße and Rudolfsstraße formed the corner where our restaurant and home were, and the third street was the Hochfortestraße. At the corner of Hochfortestraße and Königsstraße was their bakery. My parents ordered all of their baked goods for the restaurant from them. Since they had no children of their own and really liked the Murmann daughters, they often gave us boxes of chocolates and baked goods. Later, once the war started, these items were often nowhere else to be found, but the Wenzels still surprised us with these treats. I had to pass their store when I walked to my Hitler Youth meetings, and each time I would take along five *Pfennig*, go into the store, and buy a hard roll to eat on my way. One afternoon, *Herr* Wenzel came and told us that he had tickets for an operetta at the *Stadttheater* (the city theater) and invited me to go with him, so my mother gave me the evening off. At 7:00 I walked toward the bakery, and he was also already walking on the sidewalk on his way to pick me up. We took the streetcar to the theater. I was so excited because this was something special for me. But when we got there, the operetta was cancelled due to illness. What a disappointment that was! *Herr* Wenzel sensed this. He said since I had the evening off and was already in the center of the city, I should take advantage of it and go to the movie there. He walked me to the movie theater and bought me a ticket to a movie. He then caught the streetcar home, and I enjoyed the movie! During the war, when Magdeburg was attacked, a bomb fell directly on the Wenzel's bakery. We never saw them again.

❧

We went to the public bath house in the *Altstadt* every Saturday. When we first moved into our home, we had no bathtub or shower. We washed ourselves every morning and every evening before we went to bed at a sink with only cold running water (hot water and a bathtub were later installed). Every Saturday was bath day. My mother gave Elisabeth, Trudel, and I, as well as our two maids, fifteen *Pfennig* each, and we all went to the bathhouse and took showers. We used individual shower stalls and small dressing rooms. Sometimes we pooled some extra money that we had saved and took a bath in a deep bathtub, which cost thirty-five *Pfennig*. It was wonderful to be able to luxuriate in a bathtub filled with warm water, although there was a time limit. It was all very sanitary. Each shower stall and tub was disinfected by an attendant after each use.

My mother went regularly to the Luisenbad — a spa that offered healing baths that was not far from our home. She took the healing bath, followed by a massage. I was also treated to these baths for a short period. I often caught colds and had a harsh cough that wouldn't go away. I was run down and had no appetite and did not look healthy, so the doctor prescribed a bath for me. It was some kind of salt bath and the water was an orange color. After a period of time, I would step out and an attendant would wrap me in a large towel and lead me to a room where I was supposed to sleep. The baths always made me tired, so sleeping was no problem.

༼ཉྫཻཉྫྷ༽

In the fall of 1939 when I was fourteen years old, the war began. The German troops had invaded Poland and won. Previous stories of bad treatment by the Polish against those Germans who were living there had spread, and the overall attitude of the German people was that they didn't care that Hitler had invaded Poland. When the victorious soldiers came back, there was a big military parade through Magdeburg. The city was decorated, and the Hitler Youth also stood along the streets to help greet the soldiers. At that time, these celebrations were very impressive to us young people. We were told the reason Germany had invaded Poland was because we needed *Lebensraum* (living space) and that Hitler had his eye on Russia because they had so much empty land they were not using. We accepted this explanation and, otherwise, did not pay much attention to politics.

At that time, a large canal had been built near Magdeburg, the "Mittellandkanal," and a lock that lifted the large ships from the Elbe River into the canal was going to be dedicated. Adolf Hitler was going to come to dedicate the lock, but then we heard that Rudolf Hess was going to come in his place. I was disappointed because I wanted to see Hitler in person. Of course, all of the Hitler Youth groups had to be there waving little flags. However, I did get a glimpse of Hess as his car drove by.

My father was not impressed with national socialism, but because he was a businessman, he had to join the party, and he kept his mouth shut. He didn't want his business closed because of his political views. He often complained when I went to my Wednesday meetings. My mother, on the other hand, was swayed by Hitler's speeches that she occasionally heard on the radio. She believed the promises he made: that all Germans were going to have a better life with his leadership.

Trudel, because she was eighteen years old, was drafted into a civil service called *Arbeitsdienst*. She was sent to East Prussia, but after several months, she and those with whom she was serving were sent home early. The temperatures were so frigid, and they couldn't get the supplies needed to keep the barracks where they were housed warm. That was fortunate because we really needed her help in the restaurant.

In 1940, my father was drafted into the army. Germany had already invaded Holland and Belgium. Fortunately, he didn't have to fight on the front because he was over forty. He was sent to Brussels, given the rank of sergeant, and was put in charge of the supply trucks which transported food to the soldiers stationed there. He traveled around Belgium and organized food purchases from the farmers and merchants. For one of his furloughs home, he had packed a crate of salamis, sausages, other food items, and brandy because we were already feeling the pinch and could no longer buy these items. He fell asleep on the train and was disheartened to find someone had stolen the crate. He had also packed his suitcases with bolts of wonderful woolen fabrics. One was royal blue, and the other was a Pepita fabric with a small black and white houndstooth pattern. My mother then invited my uncle to come for two weeks, and he made us all nice, warm, stylish suits for the winter. He also brought along a blue light weight fabric, enough that Elisabeth could sew each of us a dress, all a different style.

With my father's absence, my mother had to take over the running of the restaurant, which was quite a challenge for her since she had pretty much concerned herself only with the running of the kitchen. By then, Trudel had quit the hotel apprenticeship, had attended a business school, and was able to help with keeping the books.

From time to time my father was able to come home on furloughs. After he had been in Belgium approximately one year, during one of the furloughs, he acted a little strange, as though he was guilty of something. It wasn't long after, that my mother received a letter from him stating that he had met someone in Belgium and no longer wanted to be married to her and wanted his freedom. He said she could keep the restaurant and all he wanted was 10,000 Deutsch Marks with which to make a new start. The woman he met was giving French lessons to the German soldiers. My father took the lessons, thinking that learning another language would help him advance in the future. He had been in an English prison camp during World War I and already knew a little English. My sisters wrote him letters imploring him to come home, but it did no good and the divorce took place.

My plan was to finish my schooling at age sixteen and go on to the *Lyzeum* (a secondary school for girls) called the Luisenschule, which went to age eighteen. There I was going to pass the *Abitur* (the final examination) so that I could go on to study at the university. I wanted to be a physical education teacher. I loved and was good at all kinds of sports, and I enjoyed being with children. My parents were in favor of my plan. Then the war started, and I was needed in the restaurant, so I had to quit school early at the age of fifteen.

If you left school before the age of sixteen, you had to serve a civilian duty (such as helping out in a household with many children) and enroll in a vocational school for one year. Because I was working in our restaurant, helping to keep it going, I didn't need to serve an extra civilian duty. I did have to attend the vocational school. I was already proficient at all the math, language, and other skills they were teaching and was very bored.

In 1940, food was already being rationed. Every month a household received a card containing stamps for each week. There was a specific amount for beef, pork, butter, sugar, and bread. Milk was not rationed, but the only kind available was a bluish, watered-down skim milk. Pregnant women and children got stamps for whole milk. Produce was not rationed, but only a certain amount could be purchased at a time because supply could not keep up with demand. People had to stand in long lines to get these items when they came in. Fish and chicken weren't rationed either, but, as with the other foods, you were either lucky some was available or you weren't, and you could only buy a limited amount at a time.

When my mother needed produce for the restaurant, she first called the proprietors and asked if they had anything available. Often, she would be told yes but to come in right away before it was all taken. Sometimes the store owners called her. After all, we had had a good business relationship with them for a long time. Then I and one of the house maids would leave immediately, lugging a large basket or some crates to the store. Because we needed the food for the meals we would soon be serving, we had to walk past the people already waiting in line. They became angry when they saw the amount we were allotted and made comments to us. Some even pushed us as we tried to get by. It was very uncomfortable for me, but I didn't let it bother me because we were not eating the food ourselves. We needed it to feed others who depended on our restaurant to get their meals.

I also had to pick up hard liquor. It was no longer being delivered. I rode the streetcar across the city to the distributor's building, loaded up two cloth bags, and muscled the heavy bags back home. Since the streetcar stop was near our building, it was a manageable chore.

When patrons at the restaurant ordered their meal, they were required to present their ration cards. Our waiter then cut out stamps for any food they ordered that was being rationed. For example, if the meal included beef, then the stamp for fifty grams of beef was cut off. In addition to the normal price, part of the charges for a meal was a stamp for flour and butter because these items were necessary to prepare the meal. When giving the meal order to the kitchen, the waiter placed all the stamps he collected into a little box. One of my jobs was to sit down after the noon dinner time was over and sort all the stamps and then paste them onto a pre-printed form. Each form represented a certain weight of a food item that was being rationed. I then took the forms that were completely filled in to the business office of a nearby bank. An official examined each form, calculated the weight of the food and gave me a receipt for each food item. Then I walked to the various stores, presented the receipts, and received the specified amount of each food item. Fortunately, I didn't encounter lines in these stores because one could buy rationed items at any time, not just when it came in fresh.

Because the food situation was becoming more challenging, people started to grow their own vegetables in small gardens wherever they could find some space. We also started to raise rabbits. We had had some refrigerators replaced and the old ones were sitting behind our building. When the beer delivery man, who pulled up behind the building with his large horse drawn wagon filled with beer kegs, saw them, he told my mother that they would make excellent rabbit cages. He said that he raised rabbits and when they had young ones, he would give us some and that could add to our meat supply. We took off the front doors of the refrigerators, added a screen to the front, and made small compartments for the rabbits. When my Aunt Babette in Erfurt learned that we were going to raise rabbits, she said that they were also raising rabbits and had too many. She could give us about twenty young rabbits to start with, so I took the train to Erfurt. We placed the young rabbits in two cardboard boxes and made some holes in them. When I was back on the train, sitting in my compartment with one box beside me and one box on my lap, a gentleman who was also sitting in that compartment offered to put the boxes on the overhead shelf. I said that we had better not since there were small rabbits in the boxes, and it was a good thing that we didn't: before too long, small rivulets of smelly liquid were coming from the boxes. They were peeing in the boxes. It was a little embarrassing!

Once the rabbits were mature, the beer delivery man butchered them for us. The rabbit meat was a welcome addition. It had a mild taste similar to chicken or veal, and my mother often used it to stretch stews and fricassees to give the clients bigger portions. It was tedious work to have to weigh meat for each meal, but we couldn't afford to give larger portions than our stamp allotment allowed. I often stood beside my mother when she dished the food onto the plates and scolded, "You're giving them too much! Our stamps don't cover this much!" Her reply was that you had to give the customers a decent amount — they were hungry.

Additional help to increase our food supply came from various sources. The butcher sometimes threw in some extra liver and some soup bones with meat still on them. My mother also had a good relationship with the farmers in the area and was able to procure a good supply of potatoes and a few other vegetables from them. Because of the restaurant we never went hungry, but because meat was such a sought-after item, we sometimes went a week without eating any meat ourselves.

My mother decided to close the restaurant on Mondays as a day of rest, but we still worked one half day, doing chores and catching up on some thorough cleaning. We accomplished a lot because we all worked together. Then the hired workers had the rest of the afternoon off. Since we still had access to potatoes, we would make ourselves a feast of potato dumplings and a gravy made from onions browned in bacon drippings. That was something we all looked forward to.

It was becoming increasingly difficult to find hired help. Men were going off to war, and the women were going into the factories and being trained to do the jobs that the men had been doing. So, a few more responsibilities came my way. I began getting up earlier to help with the cleaning, making coffee for those who came in early, and shopping for anything we needed.

My mother also hired a cook apprentice, a farm girl named Olga from Samswegen, a farming village north of Magdeburg. Olga wanted to learn to cook professionally and also wanted to live in the big city during the winter months when the farm work was slow. This worked out perfectly for my mother. Olga also had two sisters who wanted to do the same thing in the future. She and I became good friends. Several times she invited me to go back home with her for the *Schlachtenfest* (butchering festival) when she had to help her parents with butchering hogs. Festivals like this were get-togethers by several farmers to help each other with big projects. It was a very interesting experience for me. I mainly cut up meat for the sausages and lunch meats. After *Blutwurst* (blood sausage), *Sülse* (aspic), *Leberwurst* (liverwurst), and other lunch meats were made, Olga and I stuffed them into tin cans and took them to a place in Samswegen where a machine sealed the lids of the cans and sucked the air out of them. Her mother also baked all of their bread and each time, when it was time for me to return home, she sent fresh bread, some sausages, and a nice pork roast home with me. Those were precious items since food was becoming more scarce.

It seemed as if nothing could be bought without a ration card, even clothes, linens, shoes, and personal care items. We never knew if those items were going to be sold out or when they would be resupplied. There were two dress shops that carried very nice clothing. My mother was acquainted with some of the sales ladies there, and they called when something they thought would interest her came in. Then, she took us to the store, and we were able to pick out a dress. Of course, we had to hand over our ration card.

My confirmation took place in 1941. I had begun the confirmation classes in 1939, and that year the Lutheran church declared that two years of classes, rather than one, were required. So, I was fifteen years old at my confirmation. As the big day approached, I didn't want to spend all my ration points on the obligatory black dress, so my mother found some very nice black satin brocade fabric, and Elisabeth sewed my confirmation dress. I was lucky to have such a nice dress. Many had to make do with hand-me-down dresses because black dresses were not available on the market anymore.

On my confirmation day, my mother arranged for the cook to prepare a nice meal. *Tante* Klara, *Onkel* Erich, and *Onkel* Paul from Erfurt came. My godparents from Bad Nauheim were afraid to travel because trains were already being hit by air raids, so they didn't come.

During our summer vacation in 1941, I visited my aunt for two weeks. When I returned, I found two surprises. The first was that Elisabeth was in the hospital. She had had acute appendicitis and had to have emergency surgery. I visited her every day and tried to cheer her up and make her laugh, but that was the wrong thing to do because laughing was very painful for her.

The other surprise was, as I walked into our courtyard, a large mongrel dog strained at his chain, which held him secured to the courtyard wall near our storage sheds, as he jumped at me. My mother had purchased this dog because she found out that thieves were sneaking into our storage sheds, which now explained why we were often short of food supplies even though we had been so careful with what we used. Our beer-delivery man built a dog house for us. One day I felt sorry for the dog because he was always tied up, so I took him for a walk along the Elbe River. This was very strenuous because he was so big and strong that he dragged me from tree to tree. He was dirty and smelly, so I thought a dip in the river might do him some good. He definitely needed a bath, and after I released his choker chain, he ran into the water and swam after sticks that I threw into the river. When it was time to go home, I called to him but instead of coming to me, he ran in the other direction and, despite my calling, he ran out of sight. I had to trudge home and confess that I had let the dog loose and he had run away. After three days, a dirty, stinky dog slunk into our courtyard. It was our watch dog. I don't know where he had been, but he stunk so badly that he absolutely had to be given a bath. Because I was the one who was responsible, I got that awful job. I had always wanted a cute little dog as a pet, but our situation would not allow it. This dog was as close to a pet as I was going to get.

In June 1941, my mother had been feeling depressed about my father leaving her, so we closed the restaurant for three weeks and she, Trudel, and I (Elisabeth was away with the civil service) spent a nice vacation in Mittenwald, Upper Bavaria, in the German Alps. It was a last-minute idea. We didn't even have reservations anywhere. We simply

packed our suitcases and went. As we were enjoying the
train ride, we realized that we had left the keys to all of our
suitcases back home. There was nothing we could do about
it at the time, and we hoped we could find someone to help
us once we got to Mittenwald. When we arrived, we went
to the tourist information counter at the train station to
inquire if there were any vacancies in the village. A lady had
a large room in her home with three beds available. It even
had a balcony. She called someone who was able to get our
suitcases open, so a crisis had been averted, and we were
able to look forward to enjoying our vacation. We hiked the
many trails in the area. One day we made the strenuous hike
up to the Mittenwalder Hütte, an Alpine house high up on
a mountain with a beautiful view and a restaurant.

One Sunday, we attended a church service there and in
his prayer and sermon, the pastor referred to something we
didn't quite understand. He mentioned that he hoped "that
all would go well." We just felt there was something odd
going on and, after the service, we asked a man what was
meant by the pastor's remarks — if something had happened
that we didn't know about. The man replied, "This morning
the war with Russia started. At six o'clock this morning,
we marched into Russia." Afterward, having our dinner in
the restaurant, we heard reports of our army's progress. The
whole idea of invading Russia gave us a feeling of dread. It
made us realize how deeply into war we really were.

After the three weeks were up, we returned to
Magdeburg and reopened the restaurant. We found out that
not only did Elisabeth have to serve several more months
in the *Arbeitsdienst*, but also six months after that in the

Kriegshilfsdienst, the war service. This new policy had just been instituted. We really could have used her help at home because we had absolutely no luck with the repeated calls to the employment office. So many workers had been called to service for the war effort. Then, out of the blue, we received a call that a trainload of Ukrainian workers, women and girls, had arrived in Magdeburg. Two girls were allocated to us, and we needed to come to the train station to pick them up. So Trudel and I caught the streetcar and rode to the train station. When we arrived, all the platforms were filled with women and girls sitting and waiting. Luckily, they had been issued numbers so all we needed to do was to look for the assigned numbers and we quickly found them. Their names were Vera and Olga. Olga was nineteen years old and had pitch black, shiny, long, straight hair and had a Tartarian appearance: a broad face, slender dark eyes, and high, pronounced cheekbones. Vera was seventeen years old and had long curly brown hair with a European look. Both, when we first met them, wore babushkas (scarves tied around their heads, knotted in the front) and their faded dresses were worn very loosely and looked almost like nightgowns. This was all they owned and had with them; no luggage at all. They could speak a little German that they had learned in school, so we were able to communicate somewhat. Several times they mentioned, *"Stalin nichts gut, Stalin nichts gut. Hitler gut"* (Stalin not good, Hitler good). They smelled bad, so the first thing we did when we came home was to prepare a bath for them, and then we fed them.

It turned out that they were very nice and so very thankful for every little thing we did for them. We gave them some of our underwear, some of our old dresses, and a coat for each. We also gave them a room on the top floor with comfortable beds and dressers. They thought they were in heaven. They were hard, dependable workers, and our arrangement with them could not have worked out better for all concerned. They stayed with us for two years.

Both girls had uniquely shiny hair, but it was hidden under their babushkas. They only wore the babushkas, with their hair in buns on top of their heads. They left them this way until they could wash their hair. And they only washed their hair after they had collected enough rain water in buckets that had been set out. Sometimes this stretched on for quite a while, but they said the rain water was what made their hair so shiny. They would not use the water piped in from the city water line.

❧

When I turned seventeen in 1942, my mother enrolled me in a business school. She felt bad that I had to suspend my regular schooling and wanted me to get some further education. She also thought that I might have to replace Trudel, who at the time was taking care of the business side of the restaurant. She was four years older than me and, if she met someone and wanted to get married, someone needed to be able to carry on her job. The course that I took lasted half a year, but we had to learn the same amount of information that had been previously taught in two years. It was very intense. The school day went from 8:00 a.m. to 2:00 p.m. My fellow classmates were wounded soldiers who could no longer serve in the military and other young women like me. I wanted to continue to learn English since I had already learned some, but they could not find a teacher to teach that subject. The previous teacher had been drafted into the army to serve as a translator.

On our first day, I befriended another young lady and we sat on the back bench of the classroom. After the director of the school introduced the instructor, she said that all the students should move toward the front benches, especially the two young ladies sitting in the back. We ended up having to sit clear in the front of the class! The classes were held in a building that had a terrace on the roof. During our breaks, we could go up there and enjoy the small trees and bushes planted in containers and also the view of the rooftops of Magdeburg.

I found the school subjects very interesting. I studied business history throughout the world, geography, business vocabulary, typing, bookkeeping, and stenography. I had a head start in stenography because I had already taken it as an extra elective at the vocational school. We learned typing in a unique way: we had to type to the beat of music. If you typed too slowly, you got all messed up. Normally students received ledger books in the bookkeeping classes, but these were no longer available, and we had to make our own "home-made" ones. For any type of ledger that we learned about, we had to draw our own lines to duplicate what the actual ledger page would look like. This took a lot of extra time. Except for breaks to help in the restaurant, I spent most days working on my classwork until almost midnight.

At this time, Elisabeth was finishing up her war service (*Kriegshilfsdienst*) working with the Red Cross. Her job was to work in the hospital, accompanying the doctors and recording what they were saying about each patient. She liked her job very much.

The days were filled with my studies and helping in the restaurant. There were also bright spots. The Wenzels liked us girls so much that sometimes when they had extra tickets to the opera or to the theater, they would invite one of us to go with them. That was always a treat. They knew and introduced us to a piano teacher, an older gentleman who had studied piano under a local, well-known composer, Max Reger. This gentleman lived in our area, and took Elisabeth and me on as piano students. We liked it very much and learned a lot. He was also a composer, and we enjoyed listening to him play for us on his beautiful grand piano after our lessons were done. Unfortunately, after six months he was called to service by the military. He had to lead an opera group who traveled to the front lines to entertain the troops.

In the summer of 1942 we closed the restaurant again and took a three-week vacation. We sent Olga and Vera to help our friends, the other Olga's parents, on their farm while we were gone. This time we went to the Black Forest. Elisabeth was able to join us, and the dentist's wife, who lived above us, also joined us. We hiked a lot, often to the Titisee, where we rowed a small boat around in the lake. Once we hiked to the top of the Feldberg, the highest mountain in the area. There was a swimming pool near our hotel, so we could swim both there and in the lake. One day, we were told that there was a *Hütte* (a hut) quite a long hike away, and a shot of *Schwarzwalder Kirshwasser* (very strong spirit) was given to those who made it there. Since alcohol was next to impossible to get any more, we decided that we had to go! We made it and got our shot and pretended that it had made us drunk as we hiked back. We had so much fun with that little game that the hike back went by fast. A family with two sons our age was also staying in the hotel.

We didn't particularly like these fellows, but they took a shine to Elisabeth and seemed to show up everywhere that we were. They asked if they could go hiking with us and we ended up doing a lot of activities together.

꧁꧂

A short time later, my mother became sick, and we had to close the restaurant again. We also had to let all of our employees go. She spent one week in the hospital, and then Elisabeth accompanied her to Bad Nauheim for a three week stay. During their stay in Bad Nauheim, Elisabeth and my mother took strolls as my mother's health improved. During one of these strolls, Elisabeth met Hans Max Sabokath and was enamored with him. My mother confided during several phone conversations that she wasn't very happy about this. She had already picked out the young man whom she wanted Elisabeth to marry: Wilhelm Kühner, a very nice, fun-loving guy whom we all liked and who could liven up a gathering with his outgoing personality and quick wit. She also felt that Hans Max was too old for Elisabeth because he was ten years older than she was. At the time, we couldn't help Elisabeth since we hadn't met him.

After two weeks of being closed, Trudel went to the employment office to hire a new cook and was lucky to find and hire one from Belgium, but he wanted to begin right away. In order to avoid losing him, she opened the restaurant two weeks early and ran it herself. I had just finished the final exams of my classes and was able to take several days off to help her. Our apprentice also came back, as well as the Russian girls, so she had all the help she needed.

After I returned to my school, the other students said that the test results had been released and that I was the only one that had received a 1 on the math part of the exam. I didn't believe them and thought they were just teasing me. However, when the teacher entered the room, she asked me to stand up and congratulated me on the fine work I had done in math. She handed out the report cards, along with several certificates, and I did receive a 1 in math, a difficult grade to achieve. After that, we all went our separate ways, and I was again able to give Trudel my full-time help.

We loved our new cook, Napoleon. He had a great sense of humor and, with his broken Belgium-accented German, he kept us laughing. One afternoon Trudel and I were sitting in our living room when we heard a knock on the door to the restaurant. It was Napoleon holding two plates filled with small pieces of something breaded and deep fried. He had made something special for us that he thought we would enjoy. Whatever it was, it was delicious. When we were finished he told us that it was fried brain! He continued to make us little surprises, but we were cautious after eating brain.

Part of the training for young soldiers was a driving school to learn to drive the large military trucks. They practiced driving by heading out into the countryside. Along the way, they would stop by the restaurant for a bite to eat. My mother felt sorry for these young men and she often gave them extra food, even though food was becoming scarcer. They loved coming in and began to call her *Muttchen* (a pet name for mother). Then she had an idea: she asked them if they would stop at the farm in Samswegen, since they were just driving around the country side anyway, and pick up potatoes. The farm had plenty of potatoes, but we had no means to get them. They were happy to do this, and it really helped to supplement our meals.

4

SERVING IN THE
RED CROSS
MAGDEBURG, 1943

B y 1943, young Germans had to quickly become adults. Young men could not avoid serving in the military and were drafted before they could finish their education. Young women were not drafted for military service but were now required to serve in the Kriegshilfsdienst, the war service. This meant they trained and worked wherever the war effort needed them. Family members and friends were now scattered in all directions serving their country, many dying on the battlefield.

A month before the end of the business school, I turned eighteen, and that meant I would soon be drafted into civil service, the *Arbeitsdienst*. I would have chosen to do secretarial work somewhere, but those positions were almost impossible to get because most women were sent to work in the munitions factories. Elisabeth advised me to apply with the Red Cross because she had had such a good experience with them. I applied and was accepted into their month-long training class. This training overlapped with the last month of business school.

After a month of classroom instruction, I passed the examination and was ready to begin the three months of practical training in the Magdeburg city hospital. I received my uniform, a white and gray striped dress which we wore with a white apron. We also received a nurse's cap with a red cross on it, a pin with the red cross, and a blue apron to wear when we had a dirty job to do. The big hospital was located in the center of Magdeburg, so I was able to ride my bike when the weather was suitable. It was run by Lutheran deaconesses, who wore different uniforms. When I first began working there, I started the workday in a big cafeteria at 6:00 a.m. where we received breakfast and coffee. The deaconesses also held a religious service with singing and praying. After I got my first assignment, which was on the children's ward on the second floor, I was relieved to find that they also offered breakfast and coffee, and we could bypass the 6:00 a.m. service and come a little later. Our normal workday was from 7:00 a.m. until 5:00 p.m., but we often stayed late and played with the children.

In the children's ward, the Red Cross nurses worked side by side with the young deaconesses, some of whom had just joined the order and were also still in training. The head deaconess, skinny and stern looking, strongly favored her own girls, often giving them more detailed instruction and the nicer jobs. Despite that, I enjoyed my work there. The patients were either children who had broken a limb and were in casts or those who were recovering from an operation. They seemed to like us Red Cross nurses better. We were mostly young, nice-looking girls, and the deaconesses were, for the most part, rather homely. Besides cleaning up the children's messes, we enjoyed feeding them, giving them baths, and making them comfortable. At night, we sang or read to them to help them go to sleep, and often they would want to give us an extra hug. They missed their mothers, as the parents were not allowed to visit their children while they were in the hospital due to fear of spreading germs.

One night, as I was leaving, I heard a voice from the far end of the ward calling, "*Schwester Leni, Schwester Leni, komm doch mal her.*" (Nurse Leni, Nurse Leni, come here once.) It was a sweet little boy. I went to him, and he said, "Schwester Leni, ich wollt' Dir nur sagen, ich hab' Dich so lieb!" (Nurse Leni, I only wanted to tell you I love you so much!), then he stood up and gave me the biggest hug.

There were also cleaning women working in the ward. One of these ladies gathered the milk at night that the children didn't drink, let it turn sour and made a soft cheese from it. She then brought this *Kochkäse* in for the rest of us to enjoy. That was such a treat since we were already feeling the pinch of less food at home.

Easter was approaching. The hospital had procured some Easter candy and chocolate rabbits, and Easter eggs were cooked and colored in the hospital kitchen. We then made a little nest of green grass on plates on which we placed the goodies. The head deaconess also wanted to put a little card on each plate and asked if anyone could draw a little picture on the cards, so I volunteered. I drew a couple and showed them to her. She was so impressed with my little Easter bunny drawings that I spent the rest of that Saturday morning drawing and coloring those cards. On Easter morning, we distributed the plates and saw joy on those little children's faces.

One late afternoon, as I walked through our house door after having worked at the hospital, Trudel stopped me at the door and whispered that Elisabeth's friend was there. I pretended to need something from the room where they were sitting so I could meet him. He was wearing a crisp looking military uniform, and my first impression was that he wouldn't be my type. But, after we were introduced and we all sat together in conversation, I felt that he was very nice. One thing was certain: Elisabeth was in love.

After four weeks in the children's ward, I was transferred to the men's ward on the first floor. At this time, I received orders to serve as an army nurse after my training ended. With my orders came an identification booklet containing my picture and an armband with a Red Cross and the words, "Protected by the Geneva Convention" printed on it. The head deaconess in this ward, Sister Gertrud, was chubby and cheerful, a nice contrast to the previous deaconess. The patients were either old men or teen-aged boys who were recovering from operations. Sister Gertrud was angry that we had been denied the extra instruction and practice (like giving shots, wrapping wounds properly, and other basic skills) that we should have had in our first four weeks, so she taught us. She pulled me into a room, and there lay a thin, old man with leathery skin. She introduced me to him and explained that I would be giving him his shot today. I was apprehensive but when it was finished, he complimented me and said I could give him his shots every day! Fortunately, we did not have to deal with bedpans and personal things. There were male nurses who did that.

After four weeks in the men's ward, I was transferred to a hospital for patients convalescing from infectious diseases. They had recovered but were being quarantined, just to be safe. Here we learned how to protect ourselves from infectious situations. This hospital was a branch of the city hospital and had been a school before it was converted. It was on the northern outskirts of the city. Before, it had only taken me a short time to ride my bike to work, but now I had to pedal hard for thirty minutes to get there. When the weather was bad, I took the street car, but that took fifteen minutes longer. There was no direct connection. I would have to take several routes and then walk the last stretch.

The work there was easy because the patients weren't really sick anymore, but one time many of the patients in the women's wing began to complain that their heads were itching. We checked everyone's heads for lice and found a Belgian woman's hair thick with lice and their eggs. It was so bad that we had to shave her head. We lathered the heads of all the other women with a special cream and wrapped them in bandages. Following a bath in a special disinfectant solution, they were taken to a new, clean room, and the old one was disinfected. That was quite a project. We nurses also began to itch, but it was only in our heads, not on our heads. We wore nurse's caps that protected us, somewhat.

One good thing about working for the Red Cross was that they gave us our meals. Although the quantity was meager, it meant that I didn't have to use any of our rationing cards.

In mid-June, I was sent to my first assignment in the newly built military hospital in Magdeburg. It was a large, long, gray, three story stucco building. I was extremely lucky to be able to stay close to home. I could have been sent anywhere in Germany, even to the front. At the hospital, I was assigned to a ward where the patients were sick, not injured. The work was easy, but our head nurse, Nurse Ilse, behaved very strangely. One time, in the room where we brought our lunches and ate together at a large, round table, she suddenly announced, "Nurse Leni, come sit by me. I don't want to have to have to sit by Nurse Gertrud." I complied, and I knew that Gertrud wouldn't mind because we had become good friends. Nurse Ilse also didn't like some of the young male patients and gave orders that no nurse was to talk to them! Another time, a major, who frequented our restaurant and who found out from my mother that I was a Red Cross nurse at the military hospital, decided to pay a visit to my ward. He had come to visit a friend of his who was one of the hospital administrators. He was older and married, so he had no designs on me. It was a matter of wanting to observe how the military hospital was run and what the Red Cross nurses were doing there. After showing him around, I accompanied him to the entrance of our ward. When I came back, Gertrud took me aside and told me that Nurse Ilse was angry and was telling the other nurses that I was keeping company with married men. She had also been spreading vicious, untrue gossip about another nurse, Nurse Inge. Inge and I had both had it. We went to the head nurse of the hospital, and she heard our complaints. The next day we found out that we had been transferred to a different floor.

This ward had severely injured soldiers who couldn't get out of bed or needed help feeding themselves. Because attacks near Magdeburg were becoming more frequent, all of the patients had been moved to the basement of the hospital. That meant that we nurses were walking on cement all day long, and at the end of the day, our feet were sore.

At first, being the newcomer, I was given the jobs that no one else wanted to do. One time-consuming job that I did every morning was washing the bandages. It involved soaking them in a strong, pungent disinfectant, boiling them, hand washing and rinsing them, and then hanging them up to dry in the bathroom. Often, the other nurses had already returned from their lunch hour and were enjoying some relaxation and coffee while I was still working with the bandages. I didn't complain because I thought this was just one of my duties. But one day, the head nurse, Hannah, came in and said that she had noticed that I was always washing the bandages, and asked if it was because I liked that job so much. I answered that I thought it was my duty. She replied that this was a job everyone was supposed to take turns doing, and because I had done it so often, I wouldn't have to do it again until all the others had taken their turns several times. After that, I had quite a nice variety of jobs, and the older nurses didn't try anything like that again.

Being eighteen years old, I was the youngest of the eight nurses working the long hallway of the ward. Another nurse, Marilyn, who was a few years older than me, took me under her wing. She and I struck up a friendship because we took the same street car to and from our homes. One would never have guessed she lived in an expensive villa. Her father was one of the wealthiest men in Madgeburg, but she was very down to earth, hard-working, and very nice.

Feeding all the patients was quite an operation. We placed wide, wooden planks on a gurney on which we set stacks of plates, silverware, and big kettles of food brought down from the kitchen. Then we were able to wheel this down the hallway. One nurse would fill the plate, and another would bring it to the patient. The food consisted of hearty soups, casseroles, and sometimes meat, potatoes, and vegetables.

We had very few deaths on our ward. Nevertheless, when it did happen, it hit us hard because these men were oftentimes young and had their lives cut short. We got to know them because we cared for them, encouraged them, tried to cheer them up, and comforted them.

Our workforce was divided in such a way that two nurses worked one room. Another nurse and I had a room of four officers. The fact that I had a room of officers was a compliment to me. The better nurses were assigned to them so that they could get the highest quality of care. One of the officers had a bullet wound in his neck. His neck was heavily bandaged, and he was not allowed to move his head, so he had to be fed. Another had lost both hands during a training exercise. We fed him, washed him, and kept his sheets clean. Despite his condition, he was always pleasant and thankful for everything we did. A third officer, Eberhard, had a bullet wound in his arm that would not heal. I suspected that he irritated it purposely so that he wouldn't be sent back to the front. He eventually was released. The fourth officer was a very quiet older man who had been there a while and was already able to get up, walk around, and take his own baths. Each ward also had army medics who helped with the patients' toilet needs, gave them baths, and helped us lift them when necessary.

Afternoons were less hectic because visitors could come, and the men had girlfriends or wives who came to see them. Whenever we had some free time, we looked to see if we could help out another nurse. If we were on dinner duty, we got off at 6:00 p.m.; otherwise, we worked until 9:00 p.m. Our noon dinner break was three hours long — a down time because many patients were napping at that time. During that time, some nurses went to their rooms (those who had to live there because their homes were too far away). Others took walks or went shopping. I sometimes went home or went out to the veranda that stretched along the length of the south side of the building. All of the rooms on that side accessed the veranda, and some of us went into an extra room that wasn't being used or continued to stay outside when the weather was nice. I liked to sit in the sun, read books, relax, write letters, or just talk with the other nurses. Sometimes several nurses took the men, who could hobble along or walk on crutches, to the streetcar stop to go to the movies or to the theater. There was always a long line before the start of a movie or a performance, but we were always allowed to walk right in and didn't have to stand in line when injured soldiers were with us. In the evenings, before we went home, we distributed the evening meal (often just a sandwich), and the head nurse gave each patient his evening medication. We also made sure the bed linens were straightened so that they could sleep well, rubbed salve on their bed sores, and also distributed red wine to those who had lost a lot of blood or needed help to fall asleep. The salve smelled strong and irritated the other nurses' hands, so I was the only one who could stand to work with it. When I worked late, I applied the salve to about thirty individuals.

Getting home at night was somewhat difficult. At this time, the city was in a total blackout. The streetcars were dark, and when there wasn't any light from the moon, I had to use a small flashlight that I carried in my pocket to light my steps. Once I was home, I could put up my swollen feet and relax a little. Looking forward to a good night's sleep was a thing of the past because too often, we were awakened by air raid sirens and had to leave our warm beds. Luckily, the northern part of Magdeburg, where we lived, had not yet been hit, and most of the planes were heading for Berlin.

During one of the attacks, several American planes had been shot and the pilots had to eject with their parachutes. Four of them were brought into our ward with broken legs. They were put in an extra room at the end of the hall that, for some unknown reason, had not been used for patients. Of course, we were very curious about them. Since I had learned a little English in school, I went into the room and talked to them. They were nice and friendly. After two days, they were removed and sent somewhere else.

It was not all hard work at the hospital. At Christmas time, the nurses practiced Christmas carols and each evening we went from room to room caroling for the patients. We had fun interactions with our patients, often joking with them or just talking to them. Many told us of their families and their homes and showed us pictures. They flirted with the nurses, but were always perfect gentlemen with me. They also took pictures of us and wanted to write to us after they were released. They would be going back to the front. Group pictures were tacked onto the walls. We would not forget them.

Only one patient, Eberhard, took a special interest in me. He had a girlfriend who visited him every afternoon, but one day she hurried out of his room crying. I was told that they had been engaged and that he broke the engagement. Several times after that, he asked me to stay at his bedside and comfort him by holding his hand. He also wanted me to promise to be the nurse who walked with him when he finally was able to take short strolls outside. I said

I would. I planned to act pleasantly and professionally, but that would be all. I wasn't interested in him romantically. I had no thoughts along those lines with anyone. When he was released, he still had to come back to the hospital on an out-patient basis to have the wound treated. He lived in Magdeburg which is why he came to our hospital, and he found out that my parents owned a restaurant in the city. One night after work, I approached our dark building, walked through the dark entryway, and as I entered the bright living room, who was there in friendly conversation with Trudel? Eberhard! I whispered to my mother that maybe he would be a good match for Trudel. He often came back to the restaurant, almost insinuating himself into our family, but I still had no interest in him.

How this happened, I don't know, but my right cheek started swelling. It was some kind of infection. It began at my mouth and extended close to my eye, so that I could hardly open it. The doctors gave me a salve for it and sent me home until it could be lanced, but the salve did not seem to work. My cheek was very painful, and I couldn't sleep at night because of it. Vera and Olga, seeing my misery, told me they had a remedy that would work. On a handkerchief, they smeared softened curd soap and finely grated onion and taped that onto my cheek. After an hour, I already noticed a slight crackling and something "working" inside my cheek. Soon after, my skin felt like it was suddenly tearing open and all the pus ran out. I felt immediate relief. The next day I went back to work and told the other nurses of my experience. They could hardly believe it. I was still wearing a large bandage, and the younger patients enjoyed teasing me about it. As my cheek healed, the bandages I wore became smaller, and it became a game for them to measure the size of the bandages.

The bandage incident gave the soldiers an opportunity to have a little fun. There was not much distraction for them as they were recovering from their wounds. We tried our best to constantly cheer them up, and it was a privilege to help them because they were so thankful for any little thing we did for them. In the back of everyone's mind was the fact that, as soon as they recovered, they would be sent back to the front to possibly meet their deaths.

In September, I was ordered to participate in a four-week advanced Red Cross training program which took place in a small castle near Hannover. This training would allow me to be a nurse's assistant, giving me more responsibilities. The days were spent learning how to bandage every part of the body and how to give shots. The evenings were spent studying or conversing with the other trainees. We lived and ate our meals at the castle. During one conversation, I learned that the young woman with whom I was talking was the sister of Othelia, the daughter of the veterinarian in Gröningen, with whom I had played most Sundays. At the end of the course we had an exam, which I easily passed.

5

GÜNTER PAUL WITZMANN
MAGDEBURG, GUNDELSHEIM,
AND JENA, 1943-1944

During these years, the morale of the German people was generally very low. Everyone seemed to be living on their final reserves of strength. Rationing tightened, and they were living with little food, blackouts, and constant air raids. There were many civilian losses and many people were displaced because their homes had been destroyed. Women and children were evacuated from some of the larger cities. In July to August 1943, Hamburg was bombed non-stop for over a week. Most of the city was on fire, and there were many casualties. Women were often alone while husbands and sons were fighting and often did not hear from them for weeks at a time. At times, they ran the business of an absent husband. Travel became more difficult for several reasons: gas for private use was difficult to obtain, many railways were destroyed, and travel passes were required and only issued for valid reasons. July 1944 also marked the Allied invasion of France. The only glimmer of hope for some were reports that a new, secret weapon was being developed for Germany.

Despite the dire circumstances, young people found joy wherever and whenever they could — meeting in a bar after their work service, playing cards with a soldier home on a brief furlough, or listening to an evening radio program with friends under low lights in a blacked-out room. Young people were also still falling in love and getting married.

꩜

One afternoon in the fall of 1943, during our extended lunch time, I was alone on duty washing bandages in our washroom when I heard footsteps approaching me in the hallway. I looked out and saw a high-level, agitated officer and his aide-de-camp. I asked if I could help them, and they replied that they were there to see Lieutenant Witzmann. He was supposed to be in this ward. I told them that I hadn't heard that name, and that maybe he was still in the operating room. As they turned to leave, Lieutenant Witzmann was being wheeled on a gurney into one of the two-bed rooms. He had been accidentally shot by a wooden bullet very close to the heart during a training exercise at the military training grounds nearby. The officer in charge of the training facility was afraid he had been mortally wounded. His name was Günter Witzmann. He was still asleep and under the influence of the anesthetic, but I could see that he was handsome with dark hair and tall but very thin.

He didn't talk much at first, but when he did speak, I could tell he was well educated. I liked the fact that he didn't try to be a charmer, throwing out compliments left and right, but that he was always polite with the nurses when we took his temperature or gave him medicine. His room was adjacent to the extra room used by the nurses to relax. He came out of his room one afternoon as I was sitting in the sun on the terrace. We talked until my break was over. In that conversation, I learned many interesting things about him. He was from Jena in Thüringen, played the violin, and had already fought in France and in Russia. He had been injured once before. In August 1942, he had been in a wooden bunker near Rzhev on the Volga River when a Russian grenade landed on the structure. A beam had fallen on his chest and he was taken to a hospital in Warsaw, Poland to recover. He was then given furlough to attend a school to take courses in architectural engineering for three months. Then he had been sent to officers training school for four months and emerged as a second lieutenant shortly before this recent accident. We met several times after that for walks or to go to the movies.

After being released from the hospital, Günter returned to his home in Jena on a two-week recuperation leave. We agreed to write to each other. He wrote that, after his recuperation, he had to return to Magdeburg at a specific time to pick up a coat a tailor had made for him. Later he confessed that this was just an excuse to come see me. He asked if we could meet, which we did. I had part of the afternoon off, so he picked me up at the hospital, and we walked along the Elbe River to a little lake, where we stopped to drink coffee. Since this was on a Monday, our restaurant was closed, and my mother wasn't busy, so we walked to the restaurant, and I introduced Günter to her.

Then he returned to his garrison in Hamburg. He would occasionally get short weekend leaves and would come to Magdeburg to see me. We had fallen in love. He would take the night train, and when I opened the door in the early morning to leave for the hospital, he would be standing there, waiting for me. We then took the streetcar together to the hospital, where he dropped me off and rode back to the restaurant. At lunch time I would go home, or he would come again to the hospital. After my work, we would spend a nice evening together. My mother and Trudel enjoyed feeding him and had prepared the guest room for him. The next morning, he would take the train back to Hamburg.

I also had a free weekend, so he suggested I take the train back with him to Hamburg, so that we could spend a little more time together. He had some acquaintances with whom I could stay. Many buildings of the city were already bombed-out shells or piles of rubble, and large sections of the city were barricaded for safety reasons. The street cars and trains still functioned, but one could no longer drive direct routes and travel took much longer. Our destination was a suburb, Landsbeck. When we got off the train in Landsbeck, an officer standing on the platform waved to us. Günter said that he knew this man from his previous officers' training in Magdeburg. A young lady was standing beside him. We walked over to them, and as he introduced his "young bride," she looked familiar to me. It was Elisabeth Holze, one of my old school friends. What a nice surprise it was to enjoy a reunion in an unexpected place with an old friend in what otherwise seemed like such a mixed-up world.

Günter's older sister, Herta, had also been living in Hamburg, but I wasn't able to meet her. The women and children who lived there had been evacuated because of all the bombings. She was pregnant and had gone back to Jena to await the birth of her child.

In mid-November, he asked me to marry him. Later he told me that when he asked my mother for my hand in marriage, she happily said, "Yes, but she can't cook yet."

Now it was time to meet his family. He had one more free weekend, and I worked extra hours so that I could take that weekend off, too. On December 5, we took the train to Jena, where he had grown up. I was very apprehensive. My parents had come from humble beginnings and were pretty much self-educated. My mother had eight siblings. The education she and her sisters had was the household skills they learned by working as maids in the homes of the wealthy families. Günter's father was the principal of a *Gymnasium* (a higher academic level high school), and his mother was also from upper class society and well-educated. His sister, Herta, had already begun her studies at the university, and I had dropped out of school at fifteen. What would they think of me? As we walked up the hill and approached his house, a large two-story, white stucco home, I saw his mother, standing on their front door step. She had snow-white hair pinned back and a friendly looking face with a twinkle in her dark brown eyes. She had her arms spread out wide saying, "*Willkommen, willkommen!*" (Welcome! Welcome!) When I approached her, she gave me a big hug. Both parents, Artur and Gertrud, made me feel very comfortable. Artur was bald, wore wire-rimmed glasses, and had a spinal condition that gave him a stooped posture.

Herta was also there. She was very pregnant. Her husband, Siegfried Grothendieck, was somewhere serving in the army. On Saturday, December 6, as we sat around the dining table, her labor pains started. Later that day, we got the news that she had had a boy and named him Ekkehard. On Sunday afternoon, I had to catch the train because I was expected back at work on Monday morning.

Günter hoped to be sent to the African front, but the war there had come to a close, and he was given orders to go to southern Russia in January. We did not have another opportunity to see each other in December. He could not get leave time at Christmas, and I also had to work during the holidays. However, he was able to come for New Year's Day. Usually we were extremely busy at the restaurant on New Year's Eve, but with my father gone, it was just going to be too much work, so we closed it down for the night. On New Year's Day the restaurant was open, and my mother was busy, but she made Günter a special blue carp, a German New Year's tradition, for good luck. (The carp is cooked in vinegar, which turns it blue.) She liked Günter and knew he was heading for the Russian front, so she wanted to do something special for him.

Soon after, Hans Max was there to celebrate his birthday on January 10. He and Elisabeth were now also engaged. I was able to help them celebrate but had to go to work the next morning, which was my 19th birthday. During the meal time, I accidentally bumped the stack of plates on the make-shift counter, and they all crashed to the floor. Our head nurse was angry with me and said that I was responsible for replacing them. She explained that I had to go to the business office and try to talk them into giving me a requisition form for more plates. I had to wait until my shift was over to walk to the business office. There, I found an older man sitting behind a big dark desk. I explained the situation and then listened to a lecture about how difficult it was to get extra dishes. He gave me a form and told me to immediately go to an adjacent room where an official would decide whether or not I would get replacement plates. I was afraid of having to face a high-level official, but I pulled myself together and went in. The official was a young officer who knew Günter and recognized me immediately. I explained my situation again, and he said it was absolutely no problem. I could have my dishes. By then it was late, and I wanted to get home. It was my birthday, January 11, and my family, including Hans Max, was there waiting to celebrate with me.

At home, we were sitting at the dining table eating and enjoying some wine when the door to the room opened. Trudel stood there and said, "Leni, I have a birthday surprise for you." There stood Günter! The train that was taking him to Russia was going to leave from Magdeburg in three days, and any soldiers who had family or friends in Magdeburg were given a few days leave to visit them. What a wonderful surprise that was! He and Hans Max also had a chance to get to know each other for that one evening. The celebration was all the more special because we knew we might not all see each other again. Günter was going to Russia, and Hans Max was going to Italy to fight.

Although I had to work each day he was there, in the mornings Günter would accompany me to the hospital and come back during my lunch hour to stroll through a nearby park. In the evenings we visited with my mother and sisters.

Then the dreaded day came when he had to leave. The train was scheduled to leave in the early afternoon. We planned to meet at the restaurant at the beginning of my lunch hour, and then I would accompany him to the train station. Although I hurried, several unexpected problems came up at the hospital where my help was needed, and I was late getting away. As I got to the streetcar stop, it pulled away and I had to frustratingly wait for the next one. At our stop, I jumped off the streetcar and ran to the restaurant, but my mother said that Günter had had to leave. So, I ran again back to the streetcar stop and anxiously waited for one which drove directly to the train station. I was very worried that I would miss being able to say good-bye to him. What would he think of me? I didn't even come to say good-bye. What would happen to him on the Russian front? I may never see him again. My thoughts were churning in my head. When I arrived at the train station, I sprinted to the platform where the train had not yet arrived. Luckily, it had been delayed. I saw Günter standing on the platform and ran into his arms. The platform was crowded with couples saying their good-byes and with parents who had brought their sons to go off to war. Then the train pulled in. Soldiers were hanging from the train windows, cheering and waving. They had been drinking, trying to make the best of their situation. There were girls and women on the platform also waving and smiling back and cheering them on. Inwardly, we all felt terrible, but we couldn't stand there with tears running down our cheeks. We wanted to show our men encouragement. The soldiers, too, knew they were heading into a terrible situation — if not death, then the possibility of being taken prisoner or getting wounded. We had heard rumors of how ruthless the Russians were. But we all tried to put on a brave show. We all waved until we could no longer see them. I then had to go back to the hospital, which was good therapy for me. I stayed very busy. Helping those who were wounded brought me joy.

During this time, I had an inner strength that I found unbelievable. I felt like I could face anything. I didn't get depressed or stand around moping. I tackled the tasks at hand and held on to hope. Hope was what gave me my strength.

In February 1944, I didn't receive any mail from Günter. One week passed. Then a second week passed. And a third one passed without a word. I did receive a message that a soldier, to whom I had been writing as part of a letter-writing project to keep soldiers' spirits up, had fallen in battle. I was writing letters to many old school friends who had requested them while they were serving away from home. One was returned with "missing in action," and another for an only son of a family in the neighborhood was returned with "killed in action" scrawled on the envelope. Others were returned with the message, "died for Germany." Of course, I began to worry. Talking to my sisters and fellow nurses helped ease my worries. We thought of reasons for the lack of mail. A train could have been hit by a bomb, or maybe they couldn't get mail out. At least there was no "killed in action" letter, and my letters to him were not being returned. What I didn't know at that time was that Günter's unit at Kiev was surrounded and that about eighty percent of the unit was lost as they attempted to break out. In Günter's company, only twenty-five men remained out of the original 150. The weather was bitter — all fuel was needed for running tanks and other equipment — and food was practically nonexistent. Then suddenly at the end of April, I received five letters! Since Günter's unit had been surrounded by the Russians, mail couldn't get out. I found out later that he hadn't received any letters from me, and it took him several days once he got them just to read them all.

In the meantime, Elisabeth and Hans Max married on April 4, in a small ceremony. After a short leave, he had to return to the war, and after a few months, we were all worried about him because Elisabeth had not heard from him for quite some time. Then came a telegram from the Red Cross informing her that he had been taken prisoner by the Americans. We were so happy! To be an American prisoner meant that he was safe and was being treated well. He had been taken to a prison camp in Texas and she began to get mail from there.

❧

Günter and I were hoping to be able to marry in August or in the fall — Günter's first opportunity to get a furlough. But because so many higher-ranking officers who had been before him in line had been killed, he was offered furlough in May. Of course, he couldn't decline that! As soon as we received the letter with that information, my mother and sisters began helping me with hectic plans for a wedding. Three days before the wedding, Günter and I took the train to the Samswegen farm to get the silverware that my mother had taken there for safe-keeping. She had only been using stainless ware in the restaurant but wanted the silver for the wedding. This was asparagus season, so we also brought back a large box of it for our wedding meal.

Two days before the wedding, we went to the state agency to apply for our marriage license and were told by the official that, because I was only nineteen years old, I needed the approval of both of my parents before he could sign the license. My father, now divorced from my mother, was recovering in a hospital in Silesia after breaking his pelvic bones and having most of his teeth knocked out in a car accident. My mother didn't want to see him, so Trudel caught the very next train there and rode the train 465 kilometers through the night to talk to him and get his signature. Despite her pleading with him, he refused and said I was too young to get married. She came back that evening very disappointed. We found ourselves in a pinch and tried to think of what we could do. Then my mother remembered a gentleman who was the mayor of a neighboring small village, Burgstahl. She called him and explained our situation. He replied that, since she had been my only custodial parent for the last few years, he didn't see any reason why we also needed my father's permission. Also, he had the authority to perform marriages and would gladly sign our marriage license. He suggested that we drive to his home the next morning. Another acquaintance of my mother, *Herr* Neuhäuser, had one of the few cars around and offered to take us there so we wouldn't have to ride the train.

So, on the sunny morning of May 8, 1944, *Herr* Neuhäuser, Günter and I, my mother, and Günter's father squeezed into *Herr* Neuhäuser's car and drove to get our marriage license signed and to perform the civil ceremony. Günter's parents had come from Jena for the wedding.

When we arrived at the mayor's home, we all gathered in his small office to fill out the paperwork. He said it would take him a little time to get all the paperwork written out for us to sign, so we all went for a stroll in their large yard, filled with many flowerbeds. It was so peaceful that we could almost forget that we were in the middle of a war. Suddenly we heard a loud drone and above us we saw silver, Allied planes flying in formation in the direction of Berlin. We knew we were safe where we were, but it brought us back to reality. The mayor then called us to come back in and, to our surprise, his wife had prepared a wonderful meal for us. The table in her dining room was nicely set and plates of food filled the center. After we ate, Günter's father and my mother signed the papers as witnesses, and Günter and I signed as well. *Herr* Neuhäuser had brought along a bottle of champagne, a rarity at that time. We all toasted, and he gave a little heartfelt speech wishing us well. I felt very fortunate to have had such a special civil ceremony, considering the circumstances. We could have ended up in a musty, dark official's office in the city building of Magdeburg, but this was so nice.

After we arrived back at the restaurant, my mother, my sisters, and Günter's mother prepared a special celebratory meal, which we then enjoyed. Afterwards we sat together a little longer with our families, getting to know each other better. Unfortunately, Herta had not been able to come because of baby Ekkehard. It was too dangerous to travel with a little baby. Günter's parents had already visited once before, so they weren't total strangers to my family. His mother had grown up in Magdeburg, also in the northern part, not too far from where our restaurant was, and she enjoyed coming back to see her hometown. Since the next day was the wedding day, they didn't stay too late and caught the street car to their hotel, which was several blocks away.

Our religious ceremony took place on the next day, May 9, in the restaurant. We did not have our wedding in a church because of the many bombing attacks. The tables in the main room had been moved to the sides and were filled with many vases of flowers. These flowers were wedding gifts from neighbors, relatives, and friends. Flowers were one of the few things people could obtain for a gift and they made the room look beautiful. A small alter had been set up at the end of the open area. My simple, long, white satin dress had been borrowed from a neighbor. Small, sequin-like stones decorated the neckline. I had my hair parted and partially pulled back so that the small cap, to which the waist-length veil was attached, would fit nicely on my head. Myrtle, which brings good luck, was woven into the cap and veil. I carried a bouquet of red roses. Where someone found red roses during that time, I'll never know! Günter looked handsome in his uniform, although he was very thin.

Our small party gathered in front of the altar with the pastor, and we repeated our vows. The nineteen people present included my sisters and mother, Günter's parents, my *Onkel* Paul from Bad Nauheim, *Tante* Klara, *Herr* and *Frau* Neuhäuser, and several neighbors and their children. Many relatives, including my godparents, were afraid to travel because the trains were being regularly bombed. A celebration party followed with music, dancing, and a wonderful meal.

Günter and I stayed at a hotel that night. We had planned to take the train the next day to Jena to spend four weeks there. He had two weeks marriage furlough and two weeks general furlough, and I was granted four weeks off after Günter talked with the administrator of the hospital. However, the Neuhäusers had invited us to their daughter's wedding the following day and we felt obligated to attend since they had been so kind to us. That one-day delay had major consequences.

On the morning of May 12, we entered the train station with three large suitcases, one small suitcase, and two smaller bags. One suitcase contained the items I had collected for my dowry over the years: linens, china, and two precious Rosenthal bowls that my godparents had given me for my wedding.

In another large, brown, leather suitcase were all the crystal pieces and silverware for which my mother had saved her extra earnings and had purchased over the years. This suitcase was very heavy, so we checked it at the ticket counter to be shipped directly to Jena. The third suitcase contained the clothes I would need for my four-week stay in Jena. I carried one of the suitcases and had two smaller bags draped over my shoulders. One contained shoes that I couldn't fit into the suitcase. The other bag contained my food coupons, identification papers, money, my travel pass, and a few personal items. Günter carried the other suitcase, plus his smaller one. We were taking all my valuable things to Jena because we felt they would be safe from destruction there.

The first leg of our trip was to the next station in Halle. Unfortunately, our train was late arriving, and we had to run to another platform with the suitcases and bags in our hands to catch the connecting train to Jena. We just made it. Had we missed it, another train was not due for another four hours. The train was filled to capacity but we found one empty seat for me in one of the compartments. The overhead shelves in the compartment were already filled with suitcases so we lined ours up along the side of the corridor outside the compartment, and Günter stood near them. I took off my coat but kept a good hold on my two bags. Günter also took off his coat and his holster with the pistol and hung them, along with his officer's cap, on a nearby hook. Our car was nearly at the end of the train.

The train drove peacefully through countryside. The day was warm and sunny and we enjoyed the view of houses, trees, and meadows flying by. The first stop was the small town of Merseburg, where the Leuna Works, the largest chemical factory producing synthetic gasoline in Germany, was located. The area where the train passed included many buildings, a row of narrow, round, tall smoke stacks belching smoke, and raised, gigantic metal pipes going in all directions. All of this stretched on for what seemed like miles. During the stop, we learned that an air raid warning had been issued. The train then slowly moved on, since it had a schedule to maintain, and we hoped that within five or six minutes we would be out of this possible target area. But then, the train suddenly stopped. We had only passed by part of the factory area. Everyone looked around, wondering what was going on. We could hear the alarms going off, and Günter said with concern, "I hope they aren't planning to bomb the factory." He looked out his side window and then opened the sliding glass door to the compartment to call me over to look out as well. He pointed up at the sky. The sky was a brilliant blue, not a cloud in sight. And high in the sky I saw a sliver formation of planes, reflecting the sunshine. It was a beautiful sight except for what it represented. As we looked up, we began to hear the drone of the planes and "splashing" sounds where bombs were hitting pipes in the distance.

Then we heard the sounds of the bombs coming closer and Günter shouted, "Everybody, down on the floor!" The compartment was so crowded that I laid face-down on the floor outside the compartment. The explosions thundered louder still, and I could feel the air pressure around me change. It was as though air was being sucked away. I could feel the train being lifted into the air and dropping again, and shaking as if we were experiencing an earthquake. I sensed the pressure becoming greater and suddenly heard glass shattering all around me. A door dropped flatly onto me but it didn't hurt. It was the compartment door. Lying there, I thought this was the end. Just as suddenly as it had started, it stopped and all was quiet. Gradually, I started smelling smoke. Günter lifted the door off of me and helped me stand up. I was in a daze and could not believe what I was seeing. Practically the whole side of the train, next to where I had lain, was gone! It was so open I could see down the length of the damaged train. There were glass shards from the broken windows on the floor, even in the compartment, because the windows on the other side had shattered as well. The people in there were slowly getting up. All the suitcases from the upper shelves had landed on their heads. One woman had such a heavy load of boxes and suitcases on her feet that the only way to free her feet was to pull her out of her shoes and stockings. Then she walked barefoot down the outside aisle over the broken glass with bleeding feet. Having been hit by something, another lady's cheek was swollen twice its size.

A conductor appeared out of the black smoke that started billowing through the coach from somewhere. He seemed lost and shaken. He turned to Günter saying, "Lieutenant, Lieutenant! What should we do?"

Günter replied, "See that everyone gets out of the train and to the bomb craters as soon as possible." Günter's command helped him to snap out of his confused state, and he went to work helping the passengers.

Günter knew that more waves of bombers were to come and the alarms were still sounding. Some people had already panicked and jumped out of the windows, but this was a mistake. The tracks were raised with steep banks on both sides. Sharp rocks covered these banks. Many people cut themselves when they landed and were bleeding. Others broke arms or legs. Günter and I were close to the door, so we could jump out carefully. I still had my two bags with me but we left the suitcases.

We ran from the train, down the bank and over to a deep crater that a bomb had made. We jumped into the crater and quickly laid down. As soon as we laid down we heard the second wave of planes approaching. We hoped the strategy that bombs didn't strike twice in the same place held true, and it did. As we were laying in the crater with others, we began to hear the droning again and then the splashing of the bombs, but they were a little further east of us. The tanks and pipes that had been hit were burning, and the sky was filled with thick black smoke. We could hardly breathe. Not only was there a lot of soot in the air, but also dust and dirt. When I tried to pull my hair back, it was so filled with soot and dust that it stood on end. When that attack was over, even more people jumped into the crater with us, and Günter directed others to the other holes that surrounded us. Then we all waited for more attacks or for the "all clear" whistle.

Not too long afterward, the "all clear" whistle sounded, and we heard the sirens of emergency vehicles. They were coming to pick up all of the injured people. Since we just had a few bumps and bruises, Günter suggested that we get out of the immediate area. We walked down a nearby road to a small village that we could see in the distance. We hoped we could find somewhere to wash the black soot from our faces, arms, and legs. As we approached a house, the people were just stepping out of their basement stairway. They welcomed us in the friendliest way, gave us water to drink, and allowed us to wash the black soot from our faces, arms, and legs. After we had rested a short while, Günter thought that we should try to walk back to Merseburg, the town through which we had come, to see if we could find a train connection back to Magdeburg. But first, he wanted to walk back to our train and retrieve our suitcases. The thirteen-year-old son of the family volunteered to go along and help. They walked back while I stayed and talked with the family. After a while, we grew concerned because Günter and the boy had not returned. We waited a while longer. Finally, I walked back to the tracks where I could see our train in the distance, through a rounded underpass where the trains drove under a highway. It was engulfed in flames. Günter and the boy were walking toward me. When they reached me, Günter said the flames were too intense and he couldn't get near enough to get our suitcases. He did hear his pistol go off in the fire! Besides our suitcases, our coats and Günter's cap and holster were burning in the fire. He was concerned because these were part of his military uniform and now he was not in full uniform, for which he could be arrested. I was not too upset about my own loss. Clothes could be replaced. I did regret losing the jewelry that I had received as gifts throughout the years. What hurt the most was losing all the photos of school friends, patients, and family. (Without thinking I had clung to my two bags so I had my important papers and, of course, the shoes!) There was nothing more we could do, so we walked to the intersection where the road to Merseburg met the one we were on. After a short time, we noticed a truck approaching us. We turned and waved, and the driver stopped. We asked if we could hitch a ride to Merseburg, and he replied that he was carrying bags of flour, but we could sit on top of them. As we climbed on top of the bags, covered in white flour dust, we too, got dusty. What a sight we were! We couldn't stop laughing! We and our clothes, which were black with soot, were now also covered with the white dust.

We asked the man to drop us off in the middle of the town so we could go to the city building. We first wanted to put in a claim for the items we had lost on the train. Then, I had to apply for a new traveling permit since my travel plans had now changed. Civilians had to have these permits to travel anywhere. I also needed to obtain stamps for the clothing I had lost. Otherwise, I would not be able to buy replacements in the future. The officials there were helpful and, because of our appearance, they looked like they felt sorry for us. They also gave us directions to the train station. We knew we would have to walk there because no trains, buses, or streetcars were running.

As we left the city building, the alarms sounded again, and we immediately ran to the nearest house and huddled together with several old people in a nearby cellar. It was dark because the town had been hit before and there was no electricity. A few people had candles that gave off a little light. We were only there a short time before the "all-clear" whistle sounded, and we walked on to the railway station. As we waited for the next train, we huddled in a corner, away from people, because we were so filthy and unkempt.

When the train arrived in Magdeburg, my first priority was to turn in my traveling permit to show that I hadn't made the trip to Jena and then to find a phone and call my mother. I didn't want to shock her by just showing up on the doorstep. Trudel answered the phone, and I explained our situation. She offered to send one of our hired girls to come to the streetcar stop to help us with our luggage. I told her it wasn't necessary.

When we got to the restaurant, we entered through the main room, and when my mother saw us, she came running to us, crying. She was so happy to see us and to know we were safe. After seeing us, my mother and sisters realized all we had been through. They immediately prepared a bath for me. It took four washings before all the soot washed out of my hair. A bath had never felt so good! Once we were both clean, we called Günter's parents. They had waited a long time at the Jena station for us to arrive when the news was announced that our train was hit by bombs. They had been extremely worried and were so happy and comforted to get our call.

Our goal was still to find a way to get to Jena as soon as possible. My sisters went through their clothes to see what they could spare for me. I added some old clothes that I had not planned to wear during my honeymoon and packed my new trousseau into another borrowed suitcase. The next morning we were off to the train station, but this time we bought our tickets for a train that drove to Erfurt and connected with one that continued on to Jena. My mother called my *Tante* Babette and *Onkel* Paul, who lived in Erfurt. We were able to visit with them and stay the night and eat a good meal there. They owned a paint varnish factory and through their connections were still able to get food items that others could not get. The next morning, we caught our train to Jena and thankfully had an uneventful trip that time.

The four weeks in Jena were wonderful. We hiked often, and there were many places to walk just in Jena. Sometimes

Günter's parents joined us. I also met some of Günter's classmates who also happened to be home on furlough. His life-long friend, Kurt Roselt, came often in the evenings, and we played Skat, a popular German card game played with three players. He lost an arm in the war and had already been discharged from the army. He used a little stand to hold his cards and was able to play with one hand. Another friend, Remde, was no longer able to fight due to a head injury. He and his wife, Rösle, were both studying medicine and joined us for a walk on weekends or came to the house at afternoon coffee time. Herta also lived there with five-month-old Ekkehard. We had a lot of fun playing with him. We did have to occasionally run to the basement when the alarms went off, but each time it was just a fly over.

We were often outside in the warm May weather or off visiting with friends. The house was large enough for all of us to comfortably live together when we stayed inside. On the main floor, the living room/dining room contained a cushioned couch, a large dining room table, and other furniture pieces typical of that time. The parlor had a small couch, a beautiful inlaid wood desk, and a piano. A sparkling crystal chandelier hung from the ceiling. The kitchen was small and led to a balcony. The kitchen had a small charcoal-burning stove, which came in handy later when the gas lines were destroyed. The parents' bedroom was also on the main floor. The upstairs had three bedrooms. Herta used her old room for herself and Ekkehard. Günter's bedroom had been arranged into a small living room for us, and we used the adjacent empty room as our bedroom.

The house was located on a hill on the outskirts of Jena. There was a small yard behind the house, and behind that was an open area where nothing had yet been built. This was designated a "balloon area." When incoming planes were sighted, hot air balloons, which had ropes tied to them, were raised into the sky to cause the planes to have to fly higher to avoid them. This was done all over Jena to keep the enemy from easily flying over and strafing trains, buildings, streetcars, etc. These balloons were manned by boys from the Hitler Youth. Because of these balloons, we often knew before the alarms sounded that planes were coming.

I got along very well with Günter's parents. His father was such a kind and friendly man. I couldn't help but like him. Besides being a principal, he taught English and history at the Gymnasium. Every morning he rode his bicycle to the school, and in the afternoons, he pushed it back up the hill. Günter's mother was a bit eccentric, but this was not problematic. She was an accomplished pianist and, every once in a while, I was asked to come into the parlor to listen to her play. I enjoyed listening, and I know it pleased her.

We also listened to the radio often. There were stations that played soap operas or current hits from movies or classical music, but most of the time we turned it on to hear special announcements or updates. It was often difficult to tell whether the reports were the truth or propaganda. The overall feeling among us was of lost hope. Günter was talented in impersonating some of the political figures and made parodies of their speeches, making us all laugh. Of course, he only did this with family and the friends he could trust. He also performed parodies of poems by Schiller or Goethe and could mimic the various dialects of Germany, all of which was very funny and made us forget the serious events that were going on around us.

On the streets, people complained about the lack of available food. It was difficult to live only off of what the stamps would buy. Whenever word got out that fresh vegetables or extra cans of meat had come in, the lines stretched out endlessly. In the Witzmann household, we ate pretty well since we had stamps from Günter and his parents, and Herta and I had also brought some along.

Although Günter's mother missed the king of Prussia and, like many people, she felt uncomfortable with national-socialism, she believed everything she heard on the radio and agreed with the war and the politics behind it. She could not get it through her head that we were all being told lies. We didn't talk politics much because we didn't want to upset her. At the dinner table, if Günter or Herta made a remark against the regime, she would say, "Artur, say something!" She wasn't able to debate against her children.

Günter's father was a *Ortsgruppenleiter*, a political position in the party that was often held by leaders in the community. If you wanted to keep your job, you had to be a member of the Nazi party, and the upper-class professionals were given positions of leadership. He rarely said anything about his views and used his position to help people whenever he could. In one instance, the position of another principal, Dr. Fricke, was being threatened because he had made some negative comments against the party. Artur told the authorities that they would not be able to find a better leader for the schools and helped save his job.

The four weeks went by fast, and the time came for Günter to go back to Hamburg to be shipped to the front in Russia and for me to go back to Magdeburg to work in the hospital. That was a difficult good-bye. We did not know if we would see each other again. The times we were living through, though, had hardened us mentally, so we stayed strong. We didn't break down and become depressed. We just kept on working and kept hoping that the future would turn out well.

However, our hopes were kept alive with the news on the radio. It was filled with reports of new weapons that were being developed and would be used to eventually win the war. Also, soldiers who were returning from the front lines told us that the conditions there were better than those within Germany.

❧

I realized I was pregnant when the disinfectant smells in the hospital made me nauseous. The first thing I did after I walked through the doors of the hospital every morning was run to the toilet and throw up. At other times during the day, certain odors caused me to feel sick again, and I had a hard time doing my work. I also had to save my breakfast until later in the day when the smells no longer bothered me so much. Whenever I got sick, the other nurses had to take over for me, and I hated to make them work extra. We were all overworked as it was. I didn't want to quit because we were already so short-handed.

When I first knew I was pregnant, one of the nurses recommended a midwife who had her private practice on the other side of the city. I was able to take the streetcar there. This woman had four rooms in her house for women who had gone into labor. If all went well, they could deliver their babies there. If she noticed any special problems, a medical doctor would be notified, and the woman would be taken to the hospital for the delivery. I saw her early so that I could reserve a room for the estimated time of delivery. After she confirmed that I was pregnant, I immediately wrote to Günter. Oh, was he happy! The men didn't know whether they would survive the war, so having a child to carry on their name or bloodline was important to them.

In August, I received a letter from the military hospital in Gundelsheim that Günter was a patient there. He had been sent home because he had a very bad case of dysentery. His stomach was bleeding, his body was down to skin and bones, and he would surely have died, had he stayed in Russia. At the hospital, he was being treated by a gastroenterologist who was known to be the best in his field. Because of his expertise in handling severe cases, this doctor saved his life.

The hospital in Gundelsheim also sent a letter to my hospital requesting a visit from me to my husband, so I got a few days off. I took a train through Heilbronn, which was a very dangerous route. Trains on this route were often bombed or were stopped for hours because of damage on the tracks. However, I made it there safely and was able to visit for a few days before I had to return to Magdeburg.

I worked through my fifth month even though the morning sickness continued, and frequent heartburn was beginning to be a problem. Nurse Hanna had just come back from an extended leave. Her husband, who had been a teacher but who was drafted into the army, had been killed. We felt so bad. She was so well liked by all. She told me that I should take a pregnancy leave; many had done this already in their third month of pregnancy. Not only was I sick often, but lifting patients and carrying heavy kettles and boxes of supplies was very strenuous. She sent me to a doctor who worked in the hospital and who would sign the form for my pregnancy leave. I quickly walked to his office. He signed a form that granted me the leave, and he also said he would turn in a form for a discharge of service. I was suddenly free to enjoy my pregnancy.

At noon on September 11, 1944 bombs rained down on Magdeburg. The restaurant was full of guests, and I was in the kitchen cutting the core out of plums, which my mother was cooking for plum jam. Several big pots of the simmering plums, and other foods for the guests were on the stove. My Red Cross uniform lay folded on a table on our living room with all the identification papers that I planned to return to the hospital. (My discharge had become official.) Suddenly, the alarms sounded. We quickly herded the guests out of the restaurant. There was a bomb shelter right across the street for them to run to. My mother, our helpers, and I ran down to our basement. When I got down there I realized that had forgotten to grab the satchel of my important identification papers, so I ran back up. On my way back down to the basement, the building began shaking as if an earthquake had hit, and I heard wood splintering. I felt the air pressure increasing. In the basement we heard the big windows of the restaurant shattering and whole walls above us crashing down. Dust started seeping down into the basement. Large beams had been placed in our basement to hold up the main floor of the building so it could safely be used as a bunker. A large tub filled with water stood along one wall. Large cement blocks had also been placed on the sills in front of the basement windows to prevent anything from blasting through. We had all lain down on the floor, and my mother lay on top of me to prevent a possible miscarriage. We felt relatively safe although the entire building shook the whole time. We felt the vibrations of the rumbling, and again I felt the change in air pressure. Gradually the rumbling became quieter, and the changes in air pressure and vibrations eased. The dust had become so dense we could hardly breathe. I took my headscarf, dipped it into the water and tied it around my mouth so I could get some clean breaths.

We heard someone outside call that we were trapped because of all the rubble. Luckily, they were standing in the Rudolfstraße, and because our building was on a corner, there was another entrance on the Königstraße that was open. We were able to climb out that way. After we all had scrambled up onto the street, we began to examine the damage. We had not taken a direct hit, but our building was heavily damaged. Six stories of cement blocks, stucco, wood frames and glass had mostly imploded into a huge pile of rubble in the back courtyard. In the front, all of the windows and doors were blown out. In the kitchen, the door to the back was blown away and the pots of food on the stove were filled with debris. We couldn't get out the back way, so we walked to the front again and walked around the outside. From the Rudolfstraße, we were not able to use the back door to the restaurant, but the door to our living quarters was open. A few walls were still partially standing. All windows and doors had been ripped away, and the entire room looked gray. There was such a thick layer of dust on everything that I hardly recognized some of the pieces of furniture or what had been laying on them. All pictures on the walls had fallen. I noticed that the beautiful Delft vase had fallen into a corner but was only nicked.

It was an exceptionally cold day for September. I could feel the cold wind blow through the open windows and doors. I found the hooded Red Cross coat and wore that, but it was difficult to overcome the chill in the air. I ended up with a cold within the next few days. After we had examined our damage, we went back to the Königstraße to look at the damage of our neighbors. Most of the buildings were reduced to rubble with only a few walls standing. One of the bombs had hit the side of the bomb shelter, and eight people had died there. We helped the older ladies as they climbed up out of the shelter. A gentleman requested that we distract one of the ladies while they took her husband's body from the shelter. Elisabeth was quick to act. She said to the lady, "Come to our basement. We have a little water down there, and you can freshen up a little. It will make you feel better, and when we are finished they will have brought your husband up." The lady complied, and when they came back up her husband's body was laid out on the street. It was very sad.

Of course, there was neither electricity nor gas to cook anything. Still, we discovered that we could get into our supply room by climbing through an upper window. The supply room had not only food supplies, but also several big refrigerated cabinets where we kept the meat for the restaurant. The doors to these cabinets had all come off, so we took all the meat to friends who lived in a part of the city that had not been hit and still had gas with which to cook. They cooked us a good meal and let us bathe there. In the meantime, the Red Cross had set up food stations where people could get a warm meal or something warm to drink.

The clean-up also began. We first rolled up tablecloths, blankets on beds, and rugs and threw them out the windows. We spent the rest of the day gradually cleaning what we could. An acquaintance of my mother boarded up the windows and reset the doors so that they could be locked. There were many foreign workers in the city who were looting in the bombed-out areas. Another friend of the family, who lived outside of the city, had extra room in his house, so we were able to sleep in warm rooms with electricity rather than in our cold, dark rooms.

All of the relatives had heard the news on the radio, as did Günter in the hospital in Gundelsheim, but they couldn't confirm whether we were alive or dead because all telephone lines in the area were down. On the second day, I went to the main post office to make a "blitz call" to the hospital to let Günter know that I was alive. A "blitz call" could only last a few seconds — just long enough to quickly say that you were alive, that no one was hurt, etc.

I also went to the doctor to get a written confirmation that I was five months pregnant, needed to travel to a safer region, and needed the assistance of an adult. You would not have known that I was pregnant because I was so thin at the time and didn't show much. I had to have this confirmation in order to obtain a travel pass for my mother and me. No one was allowed to leave Magdeburg unless they had special permission, which we now had. We all felt it would be safer for me in Jena.

My mother and I wanted to leave the next day, but we had some obstacles to overcome. The main train station had been hit by the bombs, and no trains were running. The station in the suburb, Buchau, on the far side of the city was open, but the streetcars were not running, and it was too far for my mother and pregnant me to carry two large suitcases.

Also, it was raining. My mother found a neighbor boy who owned a wagon and agreed to help us, so my mother and I walked to the train station in the cold rain, holding our umbrellas while the neighbor boy pulled our small suitcases in his wagon. After we finally arrived at the station, we had to wait for several hours. The trains were totally off schedule. Many could no longer get through or were severely delayed. You simply waited until one rolled in that was going your way. The station was cold and damp, and we were chilled through and through. A train finally came and it was the one we wanted. It passed through Erfurt and not through Merseburg! In Erfurt we took time to visit my aunt and uncle again and then continued on to Jena.

In Jena, my mother and I stayed in the rooms that Günter and I had occupied, but my mother did not feel comfortable in the Witzmann house. She and Gertrud were very different. My mother had known nothing but hard work all her life. She left school at the age of fourteen, worked in other people's homes, and then worked in my father's hotel and restaurants. My mother-in-law had a cultured life. She had received good schooling, read a lot, played piano so well that she could give concerts, played tennis, and often went to the theater and concerts. My mother simply felt a little out of place. They were always friendly to each other, but, for instance, when Gertrud finished a book and wanted to discuss it, it was difficult for my mother to show the required interest. Fortunately, she had only planned to stay a few days and after three days she returned to Magdeburg. She was hoping to reopen the restaurant. I stayed just long enough to reorganize my things, to leave some items there, and to repack my suitcases to go to Gundelsheim where Günter was recovering.

～～～

Gundelsheim was a lovely city on the Neckar River. It was considered a wine town with hills covered with vineyards stretching up from the river on both sides. It had many small *Gasthäuser* and cafes dotting the town. A *Gasthaus* is a German-style inn with a tavern, restaurant, banquet facilities, and several hotel rooms. At the top of one of the hills stood an old castle that had been converted to a military hospital that specialized in only gastroenterological issues. We were so happy that Günter was being treated there.

Across the valley on another hill was a *Konditorei*, a sweet shop, with a cafe. Günter rented a room for me on the second floor. It was a small, pleasant room with a bed, a dresser, and a table. He had purchased an ample supply of wood for the wood burning stove that kept my room comfortably warm. A big jar of *Senfgurken* (mustard pickles) was on the table. *Senfgurken* were another specialty of that area, and I couldn't eat enough pickles at that time.

I was able to visit Günter in the mornings, so I walked from my apartment to the hospital. At noon, while the patients ate their noon meal, I walked back to a small *Gasthaus* near my room that served delicious meals, ate my meal, and then went to my room and napped. My walk to the hospital was long but pretty. The path downhill from my room was bordered by vineyards. Then I walked through the town, crossed the Neckar River, and climbed up another hill to the hospital. Back in my room, I had a view of the castle and both banks of the Neckar River with the vineyards rising up the banks. At 3:00 p.m., visiting hours continued, so I repeated the process. Sometimes I stopped at the cafe first and used some of my extra stamps to buy a piece of cake to bring to Günter. Pregnant women received an extra allotment of stamps. Günter was already allowed to take short walks so, if the weather was nice, we strolled on the paths through the nearby woods. We felt safe in the woods because the planes strafing the buildings, trains, and boats on the Neckar River could not see us and shoot at us.

Time passed from September to October to November and the days got shorter as the weather got colder. We often sat in conversation in a little alcove by a window overlooking the river and the city, or we just enjoyed the view. We also played Skat with another patient, a major who was a pastor in his civilian life. He had a wonderful sense of humor and was so much fun to be with. An older gentleman who was a high-ranking officer in recovery always gave me something he had saved from the noon meal when he saw me: chocolate pudding, fruit, or another dessert. He said I was eating for two and needed this more than he. One day he gave me a small packet wrapped in white paper. I unwrapped it, and in it was a small black piece of coal. There was also a small piece of paper on which he had written a short poem concerning the piece of coal. The poem expressed that he had found it on one of his walks and wanted to give it to me to help me keep my room warm. It was very difficult to obtain coal during that time. I also met other officers with whom Günter had become friends. Everyone was so nice. Even the Catholic sisters, who were the nurses, were fun-loving as well as caring. When it was time to take their medication, the men had to line up in front of an older sister who dispensed the pills. Instead of handing them out, she tossed them into their mouths as if it were a game. The men thought this was fun.

The time in Gundelsheim was idyllic for us. It was restful. We had fun with the major. We could spend a lot of time together. At times, we almost forgot we were in the middle of a war. But small events brought us back to reality from time to time. When strolling in the wooded area behind the hospital we could hear the tack-tack-tack-tack strafing of the low fliers over the Neckar River. Whenever the alarms sounded, I had to quickly get dressed and join the other people running down the street to a nearby old wine cellar that had been converted to a bomb shelter. Most buildings did not have suitable basements, and these alarms became more frequent as the Allied front moved closer. We could already hear the thunder-like booming in the distance.

Yet the distant future nagged at us a little. Would Günter be sent to the Russian front again? What would happen if we lost the war? How many more of our cities were going to be destroyed? Would Jena meet the same fate as Magdeburg? But we didn't dwell on those questions. Living through times like these, we ignored the future and made the present as nice as we could. We laughed with friends, pooled our money to buy some good red wine, and listened to and danced to our favorite music. The simplest acts of kindness like the sharing of chocolate pudding were appreciated and enjoyed. Otherwise, we would not have been able to sleep and would have gone crazy.

6

SAFE HAVEN IN JENA
DECEMBER 1944 - APRIL 1945

As 1944 drew to a close, the general feeling among the public and the soldiers was that this would be the final year of the war. There was no hope of winning, just surviving. Soldiers, who at the beginning of the war felt proud to serve their country, had turned skeptical. The United States and Britain continued to destroy cities, and now they were directing their bombs to lesser targets. Red Cross stations were set up to distribute meager amounts of food to bombing victims. Travel was becoming more and more dangerous. With gas unavailable to the general public and trains and buses mostly destroyed, most people reverted to bicycling or hitchhiking if they had to travel.

In December Günter was released on a medical furlough. Our goal was to go to Jena, but we first took a train through the Oden Forest to Bad Nauheim to visit *Tante* Leni and *Onkel* Adam. Traveling by train was very dangerous and very stressful, but there was no other travel alternative. The trains were constantly being strafed by Allied fliers.

Several times, our train had to stop because planes were approaching. Then all the passengers had to run for cover. Luckily there were bushes and trees off to the side under which we could hide, but getting off the train was not easy. The tracks were elevated and the steep sides were covered with large, jagged rocks. Günter helped me climb down, and we ran through high grass and brush to the nearby trees. Then we huddled together with the other people as we heard the well-known tack-tack-tack hitting the train. On one occasion there was a small, white stucco, one-room building near the tracks, and we hid in there. Günter and a few of the other men went outside and stood along the outside wall. When the planes came from the west, they stood along the east wall. When the planes turned to come back, they ran to the opposite wall. I was so afraid that they would get hit!

My aunt and uncle welcomed us when we finally arrived at their large villa. They were living well, considering the circumstances. *Onkel* Adam's tailor business was thriving. *Tante* Leni rented out the extra rooms in their house to guests who were there to visit the spa. (Bad Nauheim was a spa town.) The first thing my aunt suggested we do was bake Christmas cookies, and *Onkel* Adam bought us a large goose for us to take to our Christmas dinner. Because of his position in the community, he had special connections. It was almost unheard of to obtain a Christmas goose and have enough sugar to bake cookies.

After two days, we traveled on to Tambach-Dietharz in the Thüringian Forest where the Witzmann family originated and where Günter's *Tante* Frieda still lived above the grocery store they had owned for years. Günter's uncle (his father's brother) still ran that store. We stayed with *Tante* Frieda for two days. We cut up the giblets, neck, and wings of the goose, and she made a delicious noodle soup with these.

When we arrived at the Witzmann house in Jena, our Christmas cookies and goose were a nice and welcome surprise. We were going to have a traditional roast goose Christmas dinner. Ekkehard was a year old now and brought joy to us all. Herta had been living with Günter's parents since Hamburg had been hit. Once a city was destroyed, all women and children were forced to evacuate for safety reasons. Siegfried also came for a brief visit with a truck loaded with furniture which he had been able to buy for her. Since he was stationed in Italy, he still had opportunities to do this kind of thing there.

We often spent our evenings in our individual rooms. Herta and Siegfried wanted some time to themselves and their little one, and so did we. Although Günter was officially still recuperating, he did have to report every day to the local army camp for light duties. He also received orders to report to Berlin in April to continue to work there.

One afternoon, Günter said that we needed to walk to the train station and pick up something that my mother had sent by train. I had no idea what it could be. The official there excused himself, went into a back room, and came back with a beautiful white baby carriage! Günter had known about this, but it was a total surprise for me. My mother had read in a newspaper that someone wanted to trade a baby carriage for a stove. She had a stove in one of the rooms that they were no longer using, so she made the trade. Elisabeth and Trudel had cleaned it and had lined it on the inside with white organdy fabric they had found. They had also covered the little mattress and pillow and had attached some fabric to the head cover that draped over the front opening. They had also included a white blanket. What a sweet surprise that was!

⚜

On January 16, we heard reports on the radio that Magdeburg had been severely bombed and was engulfed in flames. For seven days, I had no way of knowing whether my family was alive and was very worried. All lines of communication were down. Then on January 23 a man appeared at the door. He was an acquaintance of my mother, an engineer working for the government. When she learned that he was planning a trip to Jena, she asked him to give us a letter from her letting us know they were safe. He handed me the letter but needed to hurry on. He did tell us that Magdeburg was in total ruins.

In the letter, my mother wrote that they had just moved back into their living quarters that they had been able to renovate, although the upper floors of the building were still in a collapsed state from the September bombing attack. The very next day this heavy attack took place. Their basement was no longer sturdy enough to use as a bomb shelter, so they went to their neighbor's basement. She wrote that the phosphorus bombs came first. These fell on the houses and caused fires, which needed to be put out immediately or the whole building would burn. Trudel and Elisabeth had previously put bags of sand on the roof to put out these fires. So, after the planes passed, Trudel and some older men climbed to the roof and threw sand on the small flames that had started. Others did this as well to their homes. Then they sprinted back to the shelter. When the all-clear whistle sounded and they stepped out of the basement, they saw that everything around our building was in flames except the part with our living quarters, which was still intact due to Trudel's efforts. They immediately went in to rescue anything they could: furniture, clothing, anything that they could carry. Everything was taken to an open area in the park across the street and placed in a large pile away from the flames. But the heat of the burning city had caused a strong wind to blow, and sparks from the fires were landing on the pile of household items. To prevent a fire starting here, Elisabeth took some wool blankets to a nearby water facility, a large pool that had been built for the specific purpose of putting out fires during the war. She dipped the blankets into the water and as she was pulling the heavy water-sodden blankets out, she slipped and fell into the icy water. It was an extremely cold January day. She was wearing a fur coat and was totally soaked. She quickly went back, and Trudel and my mother helped her take off the wet clothes and put on dry ones. Then they laid all the wet items over the pile to save it from burning. Later they found someone who had a small truck who took their belongings to a nearby village where a farmer, who had provided a lot of help and produce in the past, lived. Our Ukrainian girls had been living with the farmer since the first bombing. My mother and sisters traveled to Gröningen where they still had many friends from the time they had lived there, and these friends took them in. At least for now, they were safe with a roof over their heads.

Of course, I was very relieved that they were alive and safe, but picturing and thinking of all they had been through upset me greatly. That night, at 12:30 a.m. on Wednesday, January 24, my labor pains started. This was two weeks before the baby was due, and now I had new concerns. Luckily, Günter was still there. He woke up Herta and, with my arms hooked into theirs, they walked me to the hospital. The night was bitter cold and the walk was long. We walked down the hill, across the Saale River, through the city and then to the university clinic. With each contraction, we stopped as I crouched down until it passed. Then on we went. The long walk sped up the labor process, and I was taken immediately to the delivery room. Günter and Herta were not allowed to stay and had to leave the clinic. The doctor said that I would have to be cut because I was too narrow, and I was given a sedative. When I first woke up I was a little woozy. Then I noticed a table nearby with a bundle wrapped in a white blanket. All at once the bundle started crying! That was my baby! I didn't know yet whether I had delivered a boy or girl. The nurse came in at that time and congratulated me on my new, seven-pound son. She laid him in my arms. What a sweet little baby he was! We had decided to name a boy Bernhard, after my grandfather, which in German gets shortened to Bernd.

Later that morning, Günter came with Herta and the new grandparents. Günter was full of joy while the others admired their new grandson and nephew. After the visit, my mother-in-law called my mother to give her the good news. Later, my mother told me that when she asked who the baby looked like, my mother-in-law told her he had the nose of royalty.

I stayed in the clinic with Bernd for ten days. That was the normal stay for the birth of a baby. Once the baby was born, the mother and baby were transferred to a bunker that was annexed to the clinic. This was done because of the constant air raids and the sirens going off. The concrete walls of this building were five feet thick with no windows. I was in a room with five other beds, and I had to stay laying down because of the stitches. I was nursing Bernd but didn't have much milk, so I was constantly awakened to feed him, day and night.

On the day of my release, a Saturday, Günter came with the new baby carriage. My mother and sisters had knitted sweaters, leggings, and little jackets for the baby from their unraveled, knitted clothing. I dressed Bernd in some of those items and bundled him into the carriage. They had also made diapers from cut up tablecloths and napkins saved from the restaurant. Our new little family walked back to the Witzmann house. The temperature was still bitter cold. It seemed that Germany was having one of its coldest winters in recent history.

On the next day, I felt sharp pains in my breasts when Bernd nursed. I thought that I could work through this, but that night I woke to a very high fever. I heard the baby crying in the distance and wanted to go to him. When I got up I collapsed, unconscious. Günter immediately called the hospital, and they sent an old-fashioned ambulance: a buggy pulled by horses. The stretcher they sent was too large for the narrow steps and door to our room. By then, I had regained consciousness so they helped me walk down to the first floor. During that process, I collapsed again. They finally got me to the small hospital where I remained with Bernd for another week. This time I didn't have to stay in the bunker because I was able to get up and walk when the air raid sirens sounded. During one of these times, the all-clear whistle sounded, but they didn't come to let us out of the bunker. Finally, someone came in and told us that a dud had landed by our side of the clinic and had to be removed before we could go back to our rooms. We stayed an extra day in the bunker. The breast infection was cured, but it had depleted my milk supply for Bernd. The pediatrician recommended a formula that I could buy and mix with milk, which ended up working out pretty well.

The Allied front was now moving closer to Jena. We could hear thunder-like sounds in the distance. On March 19, late at night, the alarms sounded. My in-law's cellar was crammed full of items being stored, so we rushed to the neighbor's cellar as a loud droning hum signaled the approach of hundreds of planes. Their house was also newer, and we felt that the basement foundation was sturdier. As we waited, the alarms kept blaring. Then, we heard the booms of explosions, felt the tremors of the earth shaking, and heard the roar of the planes as they were leaving. It was quiet for a moment and then we experienced it all again. It didn't last long but was quite intense. When the all-clear whistle sounded we stepped into the street and saw Jena in the valley in flames. The bombs were not only the explosive kind but also the phosphorus kind that produced fires.

Günter immediately walked down to see if he could help. The rest of us went back to bed. Günter did not come back until the next morning. He spent the night helping people get out of their burning homes and saving as many household goods as possible. The very heavy damage was in the inner part of the city. The target was the big Zeiss optics factory, but many historic buildings were also hit. The next day, after the fires had been put out, the rest of the family walked down to view the damage. The tower of the big central church had imploded into the main church building and caused the entire structure to go up in flames. A few of the old walls were still standing within; empty, windowless shells and large heaps of stone rubble and destruction everywhere lay around them.

There was now no electricity or gas in most parts of the city. Luckily, since the house was on the outskirts, it had not been damaged, but we had no gas or electricity. We did have running water. It was difficult to cook anything, so Herta and I walked into the valley and picked up soup from the Red Cross station for our meals. They had set up a kitchen in one of the caves in the side of the hill along the valley. The soup was often thin with little or no meat, but it was hot and free. We didn't have to use our stamps to get it. The bakery had been spared, and we used our stamps to buy bread to go along with the soup.

As time passed, there were still many alarms, but the high plane formations just flew over us and didn't drop bombs. We did experience the lower flying planes often, which strafed the trains, the stations, or the German convoys on the highways. It seemed they were constantly flying over, and the never-ending threat of harm weighed heavy on us. Every time I set Bernd's carriage out in the sunshine behind the house so that he could get some fresh air, I had to run back out to bring him in because more planes were approaching. When Herta and I wanted to take our babies for a walk, we couldn't go far in case the alarms sounded. We were often warned ahead of time by listening to the radio. There would be reports of incoming planes. If larger bombers were reported, we went to the neighbor's cellar because we felt more comfortable and safer there. The neighbor's husband was away in the war, and the lady welcomed us so she wouldn't have to be alone. She enjoyed the children and babies and played with them to distract them during our confinement. Other neighbors also came. When small planes were reported, we just went down to our own cellar.

If the babies were sleeping, we didn't have to wake them when going to the cellars. They slept in their carriages, and we just carried those down. Bernd slept in the parlor because it was the fastest place to pick up the carriage and continue on to the cellar. He was always warmly dressed with a wool cap and extra sweaters and covered with blankets because we could not keep the rooms warm without access to gas or electricity. He was such a good baby and looked like a cute little Eskimo, all bundled up in his warm clothes.

To wash the babies, we warmed up water on the grill of the little charcoal-burning oven. Charcoal was still available for purchase, and this little oven proved invaluable. We were also able to heat up food on it. During bath time, we set the tub in front of the oven door. Ekkehard, who was one year older than Bernd, loved to splash until the whole kitchen floor was wet. He was approximately fifteen months old now, and his cute antics kept us all amused.

Food continued to be scarce as we lived on the edge of hunger. Every once in a while, my father-in-law, who was retired, got on his bicycle and rode down the hill. Later he would come back with an extra loaf of bread. He had some connections in Jena, and he took advantage of that from time to time. That extra bread was like the best treat in the world. My mother was also still getting extra meat stamps because of the restaurant, so she sometimes sent us some, which helped tremendously. We, of course, shared everything with the whole family. Some items on our normal menu were turnip soup, dumplings made from a yeast dough, baked fruit, and noodle soup made from cooking soup bones, in addition to the items we were able to buy with our stamp allotments. We also continued to walk down to the city every morning to get the Red Cross soup. We no longer liked or disliked any foods. When you're hungry, it all tastes good!

It would have been much easier for me if I could have continued to nurse Bernd. Formula was still available, but I was worried about what I would do if the war circumstances got so bad for us that there was no milk or formula available or if we were cut off in some way. Every morning I mixed enough milk for the day and stored it in the small refrigerator, or outside when the electricity was gone. I also placed extra folded clothes, diapers, and other baby supplies at the foot of Bernd's carriage. I was prepared for anything that might happen during the day, whether that was running to the neighbor's basement or fleeing to somewhere else.

7

TEMPORARY REFUGE
IN GRÖNINGEN
APRIL 1945 - JULY 1945

A s larger cities were demolished, smaller, insignificant towns and villages were spared. When American and British troops neared those towns, the citizens were not interested in defense — they just wanted the Allies to take over and to be safe. It meant the war was over for them. As cities were captured, many German men who had held a leadership role or who were Nazi officials were rounded up and sent to internment camps. In eastern Germany, as the Russians approached, the situation was different because the Russians retaliated with rape and massacre for the damage done to their own citizens by the German Army. Many who feared the rumored brutality of the Russians tried to find ways to get to the West. Many German men in the eastern captured cities were arrested and often never heard from again. After Germany's surrender May 8, 1945, the mood of the German troops was one of relief. Most wanted to surrender to the Americans as opposed to the Russians.

In late April Günter received orders to report to Berlin.
Jena was becoming more dangerous, and with the Allied
planes constantly flying over the city, I decided that I would
be safer in Gröningen. We packed as much as we could and
walked to the train station to catch a train to Gröningen,
where my mother, Trudel, and Elisabeth had been living
since they evacuated Magdeburg. *Tante* Klara (my mother's
youngest sister) was also in Gröningen. She had left Dessau
with her two small sons after that city was destroyed to
live with her in-laws, the Wusts. Her husband, Erich, had
operated a successful bakery in Dessau and was a master
baker, but had to close it down when he was drafted into
the army. So Klara had moved into the new house that the
elder Wusts had built on the outskirts of Gröningen.

At the station, we could only get a pass for a short
distance, but Günter stayed positive and said we would
travel by train as far as we could and then hitchhike the rest
of the way. He wore his uniform. We had two large suitcases
and the carriage with all of the prepared baby bottles and
enough diapers to last a day. The train took us as far as
Nördlingen. After we left the train, we stood at the front
of the station trying to figure out at which road we needed
to position ourselves to catch a ride to Gröningen, and it
began to rain. A woman approached us because we looked
a little lost. After explaining our situation, she invited us to
come to her apartment to warm up a bottle for the baby. Her
home was just around the corner. While there, she asked
permission to hold Bernd, and as she held him, she began
to cry and confided that she had lost her only son in the

war. The dear woman was also able to tell us which road led to Gröningen. Günter stood on the berm of the road, but I stepped behind a big bush with the carriage and the luggage. Soon a military truck stopped, and Günter asked the driver if he could take us along. He agreed without hesitation and helped to place the carriage and suitcases on the back of the truck. He even helped me get in. When the driver went as far as he could take us, we got off and repeated the same process several more times until we got to Gröningen. We were there by late afternoon. I didn't know exactly where my mother's and sisters' house was, but I had an idea where the Wust house was. We directed the driver to drop us off on the street in front of the house. When Klara opened the door, she was quite surprised to see us and told us that my mother had just obtained a travel pass to Jena for the next morning to get me. What a coincidence that we showed up at that time!

Germany was a mess. The government did not want people traveling and creating more chaos. They wanted to control the movement of the public by keeping people in their own towns or cities and evacuating others in an organized way. Passes to travel were very difficult to get, but somehow my mother had talked the official in charge into issuing her one. Just as we had done back in Merseburg, officials had to be immediately notified if travel plans changed.

Klara wanted to run and get my mother, but we said we could all walk together. It wasn't that far. Günter grabbed the suitcases. I hoisted the small bags over my shoulder, and Klara pushed the buggy. Off we went down the main street, through the old *Magdeburger Tor* (one of the old main gates to the city), past the old hotel and restaurant, and down a couple of side streets lined with large, old, stucco homes. Beside the homes was a large, white villa with a small front yard edged with manicured bushes. We pushed through a tall wrought iron gate into a wide entryway, followed by a stairway. On the landing to the left was the door to the apartment where my family was living. When my mother opened the door, she immediately broke into tears. This was the first time she and my sisters had seen their little three-month-old grandson and nephew, so everyone was crying and hugging. We were all so happy to see each other.

The room they were renting was large and could comfortably accommodate two beds along one wall, a couch under the window, a small table beside it, and another table with chairs along the other wall, as well as a dresser and small cabinets. These were the items they had saved from the fire. The room, however, wasn't large enough to add the baby and me. Again, my mother relied on an old friend from Gröningen and asked if she knew of an available room for rent. Her friend lived right across the street and suggested we stay in the vacated room of one of her children. We walked over to look at the small room and were very satisfied. When Günter saw that I would be comfortable there and well taken care of, he had to say goodbye and leave for Berlin. He was concerned that he might get there late and be in trouble.

Again, my mother could not stop crying. She was so happy, but also emotionally spent. Bernd charmed my family with his big, happy smiles. He brought them so much joy. My mother commented that I had brought a beam of light into the darkness in which they were living. The situation had become really depressing for them. My being there with the baby gave us all encouragement for the future.

The other rooms in their house were also being rented by evacuated mothers with their children. Each had their own room, but shared a communal kitchen and bathroom.

⚜

A few days later, Günter appeared again at our doorway. After the initial hugs and greetings, he explained that when he had arrived in Berlin, he was given orders to report to Austria to a Hitler Youth camp to train boys to become soldiers. To him that made no sense. The Americans were already in Germany, and to go there would serve no purpose. So he had come back to Gröningen and changed into his civilian clothes that he had brought along from Jena.

The next day the town was suddenly filled with German soldiers walking around in the streets. They said they were going to defend the city because the Allied front was getting closer. But many citizens in the city didn't want them there; they wanted the Americans to take the city. There was nothing there besides old people and evacuated women and their children. Why cause a fight and cause destruction when there was no point? When we talked to the soldiers and expressed that we thought this was foolish, they replied that these were their orders. What else could they do? If they didn't obey orders, they themselves would be shot. These soldiers were mostly young men. They built barricades on the main street at both ends of the city. Even the mayor was against this. The mayor said, "The enemy will come in and shoot and burn everything if we try to defend the city, and in the end they will move through, leaving it destroyed. If we open the barricades to them, it will save our city." As he was trying to implement his strategy, he was shot.

Gröningen was in turmoil. On the streets, we heard rumors that the Allied front line was so close to the city that large trucks had been sighted. We could certainly hear the thumping sounds in the distance. In the late afternoon a sudden shot went into the city and a house went up in flames. This was followed with an American voice over a loud speaker which said in German that they were going to overtake the city, and if the defenders weren't going to surrender, they would begin shooting. Women and children should evacuate. I quickly dressed Bernd with extra layers of clothing and laid him in the buggy with other baby supplies and all the formula that I had prepared. We all took a moment to put on jackets because the April air was still cool. Then my mother, my sisters, Günter, and I began to walk briskly down the street toward the east, away from the city. The street turned into a country road. We walked for quite a long time before we came to a barn, but we didn't go in. We didn't know who or what might be hiding in there, and we didn't want to get shot. So, we walked a little further and settled into a deep ditch beside the road. It was dry and we had brought blankets with which we covered ourselves. The afternoon sun was now waning, and the air was getting colder. As we sat there, we heard the shooting and explosions from mortar fire. In the distance, we saw buildings burning and black smoke coming from other areas. This went on throughout the evening and into the night. Then suddenly, all was quiet; not a sound. By two o'clock in the morning, it had been quiet for a while, and Trudel and Elisabeth wanted to see what was happening. They thought maybe it was all over and we could return. So, they started walking back to investigate. While we waited, Günter and I decided to go back to the barn we had passed. I thought it would be a better place to change Bernd's diaper and give him a bottle. But he didn't want to drink it because I had not been able to warm it up. I put him back into the buggy, and the rocking motion on the walk back to our "nest" in the ditch put him back to sleep. We continued to sit under our blankets throughout the night as concern for Trudel and Elisabeth crept into our thoughts. As the first light of dawn was spreading over the horizon, they returned happily shouting, "Hurray! The war is over for us! The war is over for us! The Americans are in the city! We can return. No one will hurt us."

The relief we felt was indescribable. However, a sadness overwhelmed us as well. It was difficult to accept that we had lost the war and all the men who had lost their lives had done so for nothing. We knew so many who had fallen for their country. The uncertainty of what lay ahead also nagged at us. What would happen next? We were just happy that it was the Americans. The Russians would have immediately arrested Günter.

We walked back, and as we approached the city, we didn't see any activity. There were several abandoned bicycles laying on the street. Backpacks, dropped by soldiers as they fled, were also strewn all around. We turned the corner onto the street where the big, old homes stood, and we saw that the entire road was filled with large U.S. military trucks, one parked behind the other. Children were in the streets accepting gum and candy from the American soldiers, who seemed friendly. We continued on to our rooms.

The rest of the day was quiet, and we stayed inside. I continued to feel such a great relief, like a weight had been lifted off of my shoulders. I didn't have to be afraid of any more bombs falling on us, of having to run to a shelter in the middle of the night, or of someone shooting at us on the street. The next day we felt comfortable enough to venture out and heard an announcement over a loud speaker that cans of meat were available. I immediately raced to the designated location and, after four hours of waiting, I received our small supply of meat. Even while standing and waiting, I felt a peace and calm that I hadn't experienced in a long time.

One sunny afternoon, I decided to take a stroll to visit a friend who lived on the outskirts of town. I was pushing the baby buggy along an open stretch of the road when suddenly I noticed a convoy of big military trucks coming from behind me. These trucks were coming from the north, where the fighting was still active. The beds of the trucks were all crowded with American soldiers staring down at me, and I suddenly became very afraid. I thought that some might stop and did not know what they would do to me or to my baby. Although Gröningen was at peace, in many areas we were still the enemy. Fortunately, they all passed by, and I breathed a sigh of relief.

The Americans were only there for a week and a half, and then the city was handed over to the British. They rolled in with their British vehicles. Before they came, all women without young children had been conscripted to work in some capacity. Trudel and Elisabeth had found work in government offices that were set up in a school building. In these offices they found forms, similar to traveling passes, so they took some. Back home they filled out the forms and forged the stamp needed to make them look official. These could later be used if they wanted to flee Gröningen. To an unsuspecting eye, they looked real. When the British took over, these offices were closed and Trudel and Elisabeth had to report in again and look for other work. They found it working for a farmer that had a big fruit farm.

I was exempt from all of this because I had a baby, and my mother was considered too old. Günter had to report to the British officials and show his discharge papers. He showed them the discharge papers he received when he had dysentery. They asked what was wrong with him, and he answered that he had been sick. They were afraid it was something serious and contagious, like tuberculosis, and signed his paperwork immediately. Günter was now a legal civilian.

⁂

Trudel wanted to get to Bad Nauheim and work in our *Onkel* Adam's tailor shop. It was in the West, where the Americans were, and she could speak some English. She planned to hitch a ride on one of the trucks carrying sugar to the West. The Americans were still in the area using German trucks to take as much sugar as possible from the factory before the Russians could get their hands on it. Truck after truck rolled away from the factory. With her forged pass, she was given permission by one of the drivers to ride in the back of a truck with the bags of sugar, although this was considered to be illegal. She was taking quite a chance. There were many check points where the truck had to stop and be inspected. At each stop she had to hide behind the stacks of sugar bags and hope that she would not be noticed.

Elisabeth also wanted to go west to live with her in-laws in the vicinity of Bad Meinberg. So, she and Günter rode their bicycles the 125 miles on back country roads to the Bad Meinberg area. They were not stopped by the British, but were very afraid of the many foreign guest workers who had already been brought into Germany. We had heard of them attacking people and stealing from them. As they entered one small village, the citizens there told them to come into their home with their bicycles and hide them. A band of workers had been seen roaming the streets taking bicycles and other belongings from Germans on the street. So, they stayed there a while, and when they thought the workers had passed through the village, they rode on. After several days, they safely made it. Hans Max was still in the prison camp, but Elisabeth was happy to be in western Germany with her in-laws. Günter made the trip back safely as well.

It was not only the guest workers who were stealing; there were looters from all walks of life. We had shipped a crate with the last of our possessions from Jena to Gröningen that never arrived. We assumed that it was stolen from the train which was transporting it.

⌘

Despite the dangers on the road, Günter rode the bike to Jena to get a few clothes and other items he needed from home and also to check on his mother, who now lived alone in the house. Jena was occupied by the Americans for a short time, and they took the intellectuals of the community, who had held positions in the Nazi party (professors, teachers, scientists, lawyers, community leaders, and doctors) and placed them in an internment camp in Ludwigsburg. Günter's father was included in this group. This was a blessing in disguise because, had they stayed, they would have been arrested by the Russians and never heard from again.

In the meantime, my mother had met a man in whom she was interested, Artur Müller, who also joined us in Gröningen. He was trying insinuate himself into our family circle, but my sisters and I didn't care for him very much. I was actually a little afraid of him. He was a bragger, told tall tales which, I think, weren't true, and I had the feeling that he swindled people. We did not trust him, but we understood the need for my mother to have companionship. We referred to him as "Müller" when speaking about him.

The old pastor, Pastor Forber, who had confirmed Trudel, was still in Gröningen. We asked him to baptize Bernd, who was now six months old. Baptisms in his church did not take place during a Sunday service; rather on a weekday afternoon. Trudel, Klara, and Erich were asked to be the godparents. Trudel was already gone, so her good friend, Elisabeth Braun, stood in for her. The short ceremony took place in the pastor's office with the godparents, my mother, Günter, and I present.

❧

Even though the British were there, we kept hearing talk that the Russians were going to take over. We just couldn't believe that! We didn't believe that the Russians would be allowed to go further west than the Elbe River. After all, it was the Americans who had fought for this area. The Russians had fought more in eastern Germany. But then the Americans did leave, and we began seeing evidence that we were going to be under Russian control and that there would be a "border." The Russian soldiers already patrolled certain areas in their jeeps, and there were rolls of barbed wire across some of the roads.

We had heard of the ruthlessness of the Russians and decided to rent an old truck and drive 55 miles to Ringelheim in the Harz Mountains. My mother, Günter, and I would be safe there until we knew what was happening. Artur Müller also came along. While the two men went into a small hotel to see if there were rooms available, my mother and I stayed with the truck, Bernd in my arms. As I was sitting there, a woman approached me and asked if I needed help. I explained that we had fled the new Russian zone and were looking for a place to stay until something else could be arranged. She immediately said that my mother, Bernd, and I could stay with her, and the men could sleep in the hotel. She was a farm wife, and they had lots to eat, including produce from a large vegetable garden. We stayed there a week, and I was able to help her in the garden and in the household. She couldn't have been nicer; she gave me extra milk for Bernd and didn't want to be paid with the stamps I offered her. She also let me wash the diapers and Bernd's baby clothes. She was grateful that their house had been spared and that she had plenty of food, so she was willing to share and help out in any way.

Günter went out several times with some other men to find out what was going on. From their investigations, they deduced that the Russians weren't going to take over after all. So, we drove back to Gröningen.

Two days later my mother woke us up by pounding on our door. She said, "Günter, get ready to leave. The Russians are marching through the streets. You need to get away." She had heard that the Russian soldiers were rounding up any German men they could find and arresting them. We quickly packed some food for him to take along while he got dressed, and he took the bike and rode west into the Harz Mountains again. He felt he would be safe using the back roads and keeping to small villages. And there he would be across the "border," out of the Russian zone.

∞·∞

We didn't actually see any arrests taking place, but we knew they were happening. Günter's old neighbor in Jena, who was the fire chief, was picked up one day by Russian soldiers and was never heard from again. The position of fire chief wasn't even a top level political position.

At first the Russian soldiers drank a lot. They started pretty early in the morning because, by seven o'clock every morning, they marched through the streets, singing and weaving. Except for sitting in the little yard behind the house with Bernd on sunny afternoons, I stayed in my room. I had heard rumors of the soldiers dragging women off the streets into their hotel rooms and raping them. After several weeks, their commander announced that this behavior would stop, and it did, for the most part. After that I had the courage to go out on the street more often, especially to stand in line for food. One afternoon the doorbell rang. I answered it and found two Russian officers standing in my doorway. They were handsome men, and their uniforms were meticulous, but I was so frightened that I began to tremble. They greeted me with a friendly "Hello" and asked if there were any rooms for rent in this building. They needed rooms for their officers who were going to be stationed in Gröningen. I replied that all the rooms were filled with refugee women and children. They politely thanked me and left. I was so impressed with their polite behavior and, of course, that they weren't there to arrest me or rape me. It changed my mind about the Russians: not all fit the description of being ruthless criminals. Every society has good people and evil people.

⟡

Still, food was in short supply. It was not unusual to stand in line for three hours or more. I did this on a regular basis while my mother kept Bernd. We found out about supply trucks coming in by word of mouth. When someone mentioned, "There are trucks driving up to the grocery store," we didn't even ask what they might be carrying. We just sprinted to the store and got in line to get whatever it was before they ran out. It might be rice or noodles, something that you couldn't otherwise get. Vegetables could also now be bought from the farmers whose gardens and fields were again yielding produce. Canned meat was still available, and the Wusts also kept some meat back for us at times. The older of their two sons, Fritz, was killed in the war. He was supposed to take over the meat market, but now the old parents and his widow ran the store.

⟡

Müller had acquaintances in the West with whom he did business. He had a transport company and traveled to various parts of northern Germany. He would be making a delivery in the near future to Oberholsten, a small village in northwest Germany, and he knew several people there. He told Günter about two rooms that one of the area farmers might be willing to rent out. He could meet Günter there to introduce him. So when Günter left to flee the Russians, he rode on to Oberholsten (160 miles away!) and made the arrangements for us to move into the farmer's extra rooms. For the down payment, Günter promised him a 100-pound bag of sugar. Sugar was a scarce commodity and tightly rationed at that time if you weren't from Gröningen. Before

the Russians came, the big sugar factory had allowed each
citizen in Gröningen to take a hundred pound, burlap bag
of sugar. At that time Trudel and Elisabeth were still there
so we procured six bags for later trading purposes. Müller
also hired Günter to work for him. Günter was happy with
the arrangements because he could continue to work for
Müller while my mother and I stayed in Gröningen, now
firmly in the Russian zone.

Then Günter bicycled back to Gröningen to get us. By
now the East-West border had been firmly established,
and crossing it was forbidden. It was also being heavily
patrolled. On his ride back through the Harz Mountains,
Günter discovered a Red Cross station that had been a
youth hostel just within the Russian zone. He stopped there
and was told of a man who hired out as a guide to bring
people across the border. This man was a farmer who knew
all the back roads through the Harz Mountains. He found
this man and made arrangements to meet us at a specific
time and place. Then he rode on, avoided the patrols, and
made it back to Gröningen safely. He told us that he had
found a way to get us out of the Russian zone.

My mother hired a gentleman who had a truck and was
willing to drive us to the border. We had the two suitcases
that I had brought from Jena, packed tightly with all our
clothes, wool from unraveled sweaters, and Bernd's baby
items. My mother also had two suitcases, one in which
she had packed a few pieces of china and other household
items. In addition to that, we took along the bags of sugar,
which at that time were like white gold. The man's payment
was that he could keep the furniture and other household
items that we had to leave in our rooms.

On the designated day, the gentleman drove us to the Red Cross station at the youth hostel near the border. He helped us pile our suitcases and sugar bags together and drove off. Günter went to find the guide while my mother and I sat on the suitcases and waited. There were other people also waiting, so there were more going across the border besides us. The guide, a local farmer, drove up with his large farm wagon pulled by one horse. He then loaded up all of our items and those of the other people and threw hay on top of everything until all was totally covered. It looked like an ordinary hay wagon. We paid him with sugar. Then we stayed there overnight. The Red Cross ladies were so nice and helpful. They fed us and gave me a tub so that I could bathe Bernd. I was also able to warm a bottle for him and make up bottles for the next day. We and the other people slept in our traveling clothes in a large room filled with bunk beds.

Very early the next morning our adventure began. We all began walking along the road, not all at once and not in a large group, but scattered so that we didn't attract attention. We walked and walked and finally came to a small village. We knocked on the door of a house to ask if we could warm up a bottle for the baby. The people were so nice and helpful. They immediately invited us in, warmed up the bottle and also offered us water to drink. As we were ready to leave, a Russian jeep with two military police officers passed by on the street. I immediately sank back into the house. My fear was that they would catch us trying to escape and arrest us. Although my heart was pounding, I knew we had to move on. We also knew that the KGB had a look-out post near there and were patrolling paths throughout the woods.

We (the guide and eleven other refugees) walked into the wooded area, continuing deeper and deeper into the forest. I expected a Russian soldier to be behind every tree. We walked for hours. When we felt we were safe, we stopped for a rest. My pounding heart and fear had not abated. I tried to give Bernd another bottle, but it was cold and he began to cry loudly. We took turns pressing the bottle into our armpits to warm it a little. Finally, that helped, and he drank enough to satisfy himself and fell back asleep. The paths that we walked were muddy, rough, uneven, and often crisscrossed with exposed roots so that we couldn't push the baby carriage and had to carry it. But we trudged on. My fear was still great, and my whole insides felt like one big knot. What if the Russian patrols came upon our little group? We would be sent to jail. What would they do with the baby? After a while we came to an opening in the forest and saw a boulder in the clearing. The guide said that this was the border. We were now free from the Russians! It was as if a stone the size of that boulder had been lifted from me. The relief that washed through me was indescribable. All the people were hugging each other. There was such happiness.

The guide then led us all into a small village where he had left his wagon with our belongings. He needed to return to his home so that he could help more refugees, but first he took our belongings to a well-traveled road outside of the village. We and several other people stood along the side of the road and waited until a big truck that carried a large load of wooden planks came along and stopped for us. We asked if we could hitch a ride, and the driver readily consented. We had to lift the luggage, the sugar, and the baby carriage onto the high pile of planks. The other people also joined us on top of the wood pile. There were straps on the sides where we could hold ourselves steady and also hold onto the carriage so that it wouldn't roll. It was a strain to ride this way, but the summer breeze felt good and the view was beautiful. We were happy that we had found this transportation. He took us to Braunlage, and there we found another truck which took us further to a small village near Goslar.

There we went to the mayor's office to declare ourselves refugees and were given stamps so that we could buy food. The mayor directed us to a house where we could get a room for the night. By now, it was already late afternoon. That night my mother, Bernd, and I slept in beds that were made available for refugees. Günter and the other men had to sleep in the hay loft of a barn. Our baggage and sugar were safe in the mayor's office. He was a Lutheran pastor and was helping many who were crossing the border as we had done. Being able to find milk on a daily basis to feed Bernd was a constant worry for me. The next morning, I went to the mayor to ask where I could get milk for Bernd's bottle. He suggested that I walk to a nearby farm and ask there. I walked there, and when I asked the farmer's wife she was very nasty to me. She said that they couldn't give out milk to just anyone who came along and denied my request, so I went back to the mayor. He suggested that I go in the other direction. There was another farm, and he thought they would be nicer. He also gave me a small bucket for the milk. These people were kind and gave me the milk I needed, so I was able to make up the bottles that I needed for that day. This day was also Günter's 25th birthday: July 22, 1945.

The next day, we hitchhiked again and made it to
Ringelheim, where we had been before. My mother had
stored household items there from our earlier stay, and we
collected them. We found an inexpensive hotel, and I stayed
there for several nights. Günter rode his bike to Oberholsten
to finalize arrangements for the room, and Müller arranged
for a truck to take us and our meager belongings there.

8

POSTWAR LIFE IN OBERHOLSTEN
JULY 1945 - OCTOBER 1952

To bring order to the chaos in Germany, the Allies divided Germany into four military occupation zones: France in the Southwest, Britain in the Northwest, The United States in the South, and the Soviet Union in the East. German prisoners were kept for months until order could be restored. Young people could not return to their studies — they had to earn money. Many were just happy to be alive. Money was worthless, and everything was bartered on the black market. Ration cards were still in use but did not provide enough food to sustain a person. Little international aid went to Germany, and many Germans died from starvation. Those who could grow their own food or get food on the black market fared better. Many Germans had been displaced, and finding lodging for them was difficult. In addition, many ethnic Germans were being expelled from Czechoslovakia, Poland, and Hungary and distributed among the occupation zones. Many had been severely mistreated before being deported. Word got out about the concentration camps. Many heard this with confusion. Some believed it was propaganda from the *outside. Others heard denials from top Nazi officials and didn't know what to believe. Those who had firsthand knowledge were forced to face the atrocities.*

❦

When we first arrived at the farm where we were going to live, I was pleasantly surprised. The village of Oberholsten itself was more a collection of scattered farms rather than a centralized town. There was a *Gasthaus*, a small school, and the house of the mayor, which also served as the post office. The countryside around it was a patchwork of fields and woods on gently rolling hills. No buses or trains passed through this area, so the only modes of transportation were bicycles and horse drawn wagons or buggies. The nearest small grocery store and the doctor were in Oldendorf, located in a valley a mile away.

The buildings of the farm were situated on a hill near a wooded area. A nice-looking, tall, blonde, slender young woman with her small daughter came out to meet us. Her hair was pulled back into a bun and her dress was worn and faded. Her name was Gerda Schnittger. She had lost her husband in the war and was running the farm for her younger brother, who also had been killed (In Oberholsten the youngest son inherited the farm). A good-natured, curly blond-haired young man named Frösch, also a refugee, was helping her with the farm work. An older brother was also working on the farm, and it was this man with whom Günter had made the arrangements. The parents were no longer living. The brother was also a very nice man, but both he and Frösch were difficult to understand. They spoke *Plattdeutsch*, a Low German regional dialect, with one another: a dialect that was like a foreign language to me. They did speak High German with me, but it would have been nice to listen in to the conversations they had with each other.

We were happy that we had two rooms whereas many refugees were only able to find a single room. The two rooms had been added to the back of the main farm house and had their own entryway. One was a living room/kitchen combination, and the other was a bedroom. The bedroom was already furnished with a bed and a wardrobe cabinet. The other room had a wood burning stove but was otherwise not furnished, nor did it have running water. But I was relieved that we finally had some permanence at such a turbulent time — a place where I could feel settled in such a pleasant area, and where I had another young mother with whom I could talk. I was also comforted by the thought that, by living on a farm, we would not starve or have to wait in endless, long lines for food, as many in the cities did. We also found a room nearby for my mother on the farm of August Drees.

With some of the sugar, we were able to buy some dishes, pots and pans, a wash tub, and other necessary household items. We also bought some furniture for our little living room. We first bought a couch and a china cabinet. I could use the china cabinet for dishes and for storage of other household items and food. Günter also built shelves that I covered in the front with a curtain. Here I could also store many items, including a tub that I used to wash dishes. To wash the dishes, I brought a bucket of water in from the well and heated it on the wood-burning stove. I also used the stove to cook our meals. We bought a small table with four chairs and set it near the couch. There was no bathroom. We used the Schnittger's outhouse-type toilet that was located in a little room in the main farm house. When we wanted to take a bath, we again brought in water, heated it on the stove, and bathed in the middle of the room!

The farmhouse was a typical *Niedersächsischer Bauernhof*, a Lower Saxony farmhouse/barn where the barn and living quarters were under one roof. The front, double-doored entry was right around the corner from the addition that contained our two rooms. When entering the front, you came into a very large room where the horses looked out of their stalls at you on the left, followed by the milking room, which also served as a kitchen/washroom. This room also contained an indoor pump where I got our water. In one corner of the large room stood a big kettle, suspended over a fire pit, where the mush (made from cooked rutabagas, turnips, or beets and mashed with grains) for the pigs was cooked. This kettle could be lifted out and replaced with another that was used to boil our laundry. On the other side, two doors led to two bedrooms, only one of which was being used. Toward the back, there was also a large, wooden table surrounded by chairs and a large cupboard. This room was their "living room," where they gathered when they weren't working or sleeping. This room was so big that it could house their farm wagon as well. Above, in the loft that the rafters formed, straw was packed tightly, which also offered insulation. Beyond the milking room was the cow stable, and a back stable contained the pigs. The toilet was in a small room just beyond the cows.

The cows were all named. When we passed by them to use the toilet before bedtime, they were all lined up and watched us as we wished each one a good night. One more door led out the back to a covered area where a large, loose pile of straw was kept.

In Magdeburg, I was used to a gas kitchen stove, central heating, electricity, indoor plumbing, a bathroom with hot and cold running water, and buses and trains readily available. Here, the living was very primitive, and I had to learn some new things. At first, I had lots of trouble with our wood stove. I often couldn't get it started, so I had to get Gerda to help me. Then I would get busy and forget to keep feeding wood to keep the fire going, and I would have to find Gerda again. Eventually I got the hang of it. I had a good relationship with Gerda, and she helped me in so many ways. In turn, I was able to help her whenever possible.

I also had never planted a vegetable garden. I helped Gerda in her garden and learned much in the process. Since we had arrived during the summer, there was still time to put in a small garden, and Gerda helped me with that as well. She was pleasant to work with, and I found that I really enjoyed gardening and the healthy food that it produced.

One thing I wasn't able to learn well was how to milk the cows. The others, to whom it was second nature, were much faster and more accurate than me. I often couldn't get any milk to come out, or I totally missed the pail! This was always the cause of much laughter. It was decided that I was too much of a city girl, and this was one thing I would not be able to learn.

I realized that I was truly ignorant of farm life, but took to it happily (except for the milking) and found it all very interesting. Gerda even woke me one night when piglets were being born. I was fascinated. As they came out of the sow, Gerda placed them into a basket (the sow would sometimes eat them), and when all of them were born, she lined them up again by the mother so they could suckle. I also witnessed a calf being born. They had to call a veterinarian to help with the delivery. He tied a rope around the two front legs that were sticking out and pulled the calf out. No sooner was the little thing out than it sprang to its feet! I was so surprised at that.

Günter worked long hours. He had wanted to be an engineer and still had thoughts of possibly doing that once Germany recovered. So he became a mason, thinking he could study engineering on the side and work his way up in the construction field. Every morning, he climbed on his bicycle with the bread and butter sandwiches that I packed for his breakfast along with a pot containing soup that he then heated over a fire for his noon meal, which was the usual fare for the construction workers. At times he had to ride long distances on his bicycle over and down the hills to get to the construction site. Later he took correspondence courses to further his education toward his goal, studying at night.

Soon after we settled in, Gerda and Frösch married and continued to work the farm. After two years, though, they moved to a larger farm to work for that farmer and live in a small cottage that was furnished for them. The Schnittger farm was bought by a family named Fritgen and was from then on known as the Schnittger-Fritgen farm.

Günter's father got an early release from the internment camp and came to live with us. When he originally joined the Nazi party, he did so to help people during those turbulent times. Many whom he had helped, when they learned what had happened to him, had written to the commander of the camp, describing in their letters what he had done for them. The commander realized that he was a good man and gave him the early release. When he was released, we did not want him to go back to Jena, which was in the Russian zone, and invited him to live with us. He was going to have to sleep on the couch, and our bedroom was used as a washroom, so that whoever needed to wash could have privacy.

When he arrived, he was skin and bones. At the camp, the prisoners had only been given enough food to barely exist. If they became too weak, they were sent to a medical center and given more food and aid until their health was somewhat restored. He had been sent there once. We had been allowed to send him food items, which helped him a little. He had also given English lessons to other inmates to alleviate boredom and had bartered for a few necessities. What seemed to be in most supply were bars of soap and many had paid him with that, more than he could use. One day, we were surprised to receive a box filled with soap bars in the mail. That had been a welcome surprise because soap was hard to get and very expensive.

During her husband's absence, Günter's mother was forced from their home. She had pulled a small wagon filled with clothing, bedding, dishes and silverware, portraits, and whatever else she could cram in down to the center of Jena and had found a room in which she could live. This was the silverware that survived the Leunawerk bombing because it had been sent ahead when we took the train through Merseburg. Günter's school friend, who lived in Jena, helped us save it by sending it piece by piece to Oberholsten. All women in Jena were required to work in order to receive food stamps. Her first job was to clean streets by shoveling the rubble and soot into wagons and then sweeping. When this proved too much for her, she worked in a restaurant kitchen, washing dishes.

✦

Artur Müller and my mother married and lived in the room at the August Drees farm. Müller used my mother's money to invest in his new business, tape recording equipment, and also to buy a car to use for his many sales trips around the country. My mother had money available because she had been able to trade in her bank notes for money.

I had none. While I was growing up my father put money into a bank account for me which could not be touched until I turned twenty-one, so I could not use that. I had put my own savings in a bank that was totally destroyed and lost it all. I had also saved 1,000 DM (Deutschmarks, the German currency) while working for the Red Cross. I had put it into a *Post Sparbuch*, a savings account through the post office. Normally, this was a very handy place to keep your money because you could withdraw it from any post office, anywhere. But with the turmoil in Germany, the savings were frozen and could not be withdrawn. (In 1948 I was able to finally get my money, which at that point was only worth 100 DM.)

✦

Bernd was a good baby. Because we only had the two small rooms, he was always near us and slept next to us. Whenever I went anywhere I sat him in the basket attached to the front of my bike, and off we went. When winter turned to spring he (now fifteen months old) was ready to run around outside in his wooden shoes, and he liked the swing that hung from a cherry tree in the orchard. My mother, his *"Omi,"* and Günter's father, whom we called *"Opa,"* often played with him and bought him picture books. They adored their grandson!

As he grew into a toddler Bernd always wanted to play with Gerda's nephew, who was six years old. Bernd ran after him, wanting to kick the soccer ball with him, but was often disappointed when the boy hopped on his bicycle and rode off to play with his own friends, leaving Bernd standing there, crying. Then he had to find another playmate, which was usually the Fritgen's big German Shepard dog. He also sometimes played with Gerda's daughter, who was three years older. He enjoyed walking through the woods with me and liked watching the farmers pass by with their horse drawn wagons and farm equipment. Bernd also liked going to the Nagel's, an older couple who had a small farm across the road and who enjoyed having him around. They raised rabbits and let Bernd help feed them. When the weather forced him to stay inside, he liked building with his building blocks and then knocking down whatever he had constructed.

When Bernd's two-year molars came in, they caused more than average problems. He had chronic diarrhea. We took him to a doctor in Oldendorf, who advised us to strictly watch what Bernd ate. He was restricted to Zwieback (like hard, dry toast), dry bread, or watered-down oatmeal. Then when Günter and I ate our normal food, he stood there begging and pointing to our food, making sounds like "Mmmmmm." Of course, we felt bad for him and tried our best not to eat in front of him. He also knew where certain foods were kept and made the same sounds while pointing to the cupboards. It was cute and sad at the same time.

I had no problem with letting Bernd run and play in the farm yard or near the stables. Everything was kept so clean that there was no bad animal smell around the buildings. Very early in the mornings *Herr* Fritgen cleaned all the dirty straw out of the cow pen onto a large manure pile in the front of the barn and threw clean straw down from the loft above. Then he and his wife milked the twelve cows by hand, and the milk was poured into large cans. Neighbor Nagel had a wagon, onto which the cans were loaded. He drove the horse-drawn wagons from farm to farm collecting the milk and took it to a station where a truck picked it up to take it to a dairy. If the weather was nice, the cows were then lead to a pasture for the day and the pens stayed clean all day. If they stayed in their pens all day, the straw was again cleaned out and replaced with fresh, clean straw at dusk. Across from the cows were the pig pens. They were also kept clean. When the manure pile in the front of the barn got too large, it was taken out to the fields and spread around.

Günter's father loved little Bernd. He often walked with him through the woods, or I found Bernd nestled on his lap, listening to a story, either being read or told. Other times his *Opa* bounced him on his knees, playing "Hoppa, Hoppa, Reiter." Bernd loved being dropped between the knees when it was time for the "Reiter" (rider) to fall. The time they spent together was a big help to me and allowed me to help out on the farm when needed. His *Opa* fed him, laid him down for his naps, and took care of all his needs while I pulled beets in the fields, gathered and sorted potatoes, helped with the thrashing, or picked apples in the orchard.

❦

Besides helping with Bernd, Günter's father was such a joy to have around. He was always kind, soft spoken, and ready to help out wherever and whenever needed. When he stayed with us he readily peeled potatoes as I was fixing dinner or brought wood for the stove from the woodshed on the other side of the farmhouse. One time he came back sweating but grinning and said, "Guess what I found in the woodshed?" I looked at him, thinking, "What can one find in a woodshed?" He reached into his pocket and pulled out an egg! Although we occasionally bought eggs, this was quite a find!

He also liked to ride his bicycle for exercise. He sometimes rode to Oldendorf, which was all downhill, to shop for me at the small grocery store. Then he had to walk the bike up the hill. He was now even more stooped over, but walking uphill with this bike worked out well because he could use the bike for support. He also often rode it to Melle and brought back surprises for us: smoked herring or other food items that we couldn't get in little Oberholsten or Oldendorf.

❦

Harvest time was exceptionally busy for me. When harvesting the potatoes, *Herr* Fritgen led a horse that pulled a plow-like implement along the potato rows. The plow dug under the potato plants and threw up the potatoes. My job was to follow, pick up the potatoes, and throw them into round baskets that had been placed along the rows. It was too difficult to constantly bend over, so we moved along the rows on our knees. The earth was soft with no stones, so this worked very well although our knees got pretty dirty.

Other helpers came by and dumped the filled baskets onto a wagon. Sometimes we switched jobs to give our muscles a rest. Dumping the filled baskets was also hard work, but it gave us a chance to walk around a little bit. It took an entire day to harvest one field. We began very early, and at 9:00 a.m., *Frau* Fritgen brought out coffee and sandwiches for a "late breakfast" break. At noon we went home for our lunch and returned again for the afternoon. The wagon dumped the potatoes onto the floor of the main barn and created a pile that seemed to reach almost to the ceiling. Then the sorting started. The very small ones were sorted out to feed to the pigs. We also sorted the middle-sized and the large ones. Many were sold, but some were kept. I was also given some as payment. Günter did not participate in this farm work because he was working at his construction job.

The beet harvest, which followed, was different. There we walked along the rows, pulled out two beets at a time, and laid them neatly side by side. Then someone came through with a cutter and cut off the green stems. After that, a wagon came by, and someone threw the beets onto the wagon. These beets were very large and were fed to the pigs.

There was another larger Nagel farm, owned by a niece of our neighbors. I also helped this *Frau* Nagel out during harvest time. She was running a large farm by herself because her husband had also died during the war. Her two sons were still too small to be of much help. I helped often at threshing time. This was a major event. Rye, wheat, and oats had been cut and bundled during the summer and stored in a drying shed. In the fall, someone went from farm to farm with a big threshing machine. All the farmers helped each other out. The bundles had to be carried to the machine and then, as the machine separated the seeds from the chaff and the straw, the seed bins had to be emptied, the straw bales carried away, and the chaff swept up. This was not one of my favorite jobs because the air was so filled with dust. It was also an all-day job. What made it worth it was the wonderful food that *Frau* Nagel brought out for the mid-morning breakfast and then again for the noon meal. The breakfast sandwiches were made with home-baked bread and tasty home-made lunch meat. The noon meal was a feast of a roast, potatoes, rich gravy, vegetables, and a fruit compote for dessert. Coffee was brought out again in the late afternoon and after working a few hours longer, we went home for our evening meal. She gave me a large piece of bacon and a basket full of eggs, fruits, and vegetables to take home with me. That was my payment, and it was worth more than a pile of money because there was not much in the stores yet that money could buy.

We stayed in touch with Gerda and her husband and often visited them. We took a path along a fence row between the fields to get to each other's homes. Gerda was pregnant, and we all were looking forward to having a little baby in our midst. Then I heard that she had had a larger than normal baby, and that a doctor had to be brought in to help with the delivery. Babies were born at home, and a doctor was contacted only when serious complications arose. I rode my bicycle to Melle, the nearby town, to buy a small present. When I arrived later at their cottage, I was frightened to find that she was not there. The neighbors said that an ambulance had taken her in the middle of the night to the hospital in Melle. I went home, fearing that something had gone terribly wrong for my friend. Three days later, the Fritgens said that Gerda was back home. On my second visit I found her in her bed, very pale and weak. She told me that her husband had come to her bed in the middle of the night because the baby was crying and found that she had been hemorrhaging and was barely conscious. Because he had no phone, her husband had to run to the mayor's house to call for an ambulance. It came right away and took her to the hospital, and she was given blood. The doctors told him that he had found his wife just in time. She could easily have died that night. This is what could happen when babies were born at home in a rural area.

We made many other friends in the Oberholsten area. August Drees, on whose farm my mother and Müller had a room, wanted us to spend extra time with him whenever we visited. He was very fat — so fat that he couldn't do much work around his farm anymore. His hard-working wife did most of the work. He was also very difficult to understand because he stuttered and mixed his High German with his *Plattdeutsch*. But he was so good-natured that we enjoyed visiting him when time allowed. While there, Bernd enjoyed playing with August's youngest daughter, Liesel. Several times, when we had to decline his invitation to come in for a visit, he asked us to wait for one moment; that he would accompany us for a short walk. After a short while, he would reappear at the door and walk with us. Then he would "accidentally" bump my side and when I turned to him, he would pull a sausage out of his pocket and hand it to me.

The Lüpke family, whose farm was down in the valley, also had young children, and we enjoyed visiting with them.

There were many refugees in the Oberholsten area. They were all from Silesia, which was part of Poland. Every homeowner who had an extra room was required to take in a refugee family. Many times four or five-member families lived in one room. Fortunately, most farmers had an outdoor cooking stove, and the refugees could use those to cook their meals. Water had to be brought in from the well. Their lives were fairly primitive, but the farmers were generous to these people and shared any food that could be spared. In turn, the refugees helped out in any way they could.

The Fritgens were also forced to give up a small bedroom that was not being used. A woman and a daughter, who was Bernd's age, moved in there. I felt so sorry for her. She was my age, but she was thin and haggard looking. She looked like she was fifty years old. She told me that the local Polish people had beaten her husband to death and taken away the small farm they owned. She had been forced to sleep in the haymow with her little girl, and they had given her no food. At night she had to sneak over to the garbage pile and look for scraps of food. When she and her daughter were transported away it was actually a blessing for her. She helped around the farm as much as possible. I tried to speak with her and help her, but we didn't become close friends. She seemed fearful and kept to herself.

A family also moved into a room on the Nagel farm on the hill. Their name was Nickisch, and we became good friends with them. *Frau* Nickisch could sew very well and used her skills to earn a little extra money. She also did some sewing for *Frau* Nagel. Another refugee couple that we liked moved into a room down the road. The husband was a mason and found work in Melle. Another very nice young family named

Rindfleisch lived directly in the village of Oberholsten, and we became good friends with them as well.

With these friends, we formed a *Sängerverein*, a singing club. We met one evening a week in a large room in the local *Gasthaus*. Many from the surrounding area, even beyond the Oberholsten area, joined us until we were a group of thirty. Other areas also had these singing clubs, and once a year they all got together for a big singing festival. The location of these festivals rotated, and Oberholsten hosted it one year. The men erected a big tent on a meadow outside the village for this occasion. Many of the songs that were sung were folksongs from the homelands that the refugees had left behind.

Of course, there were also many conversations and stories of the refugees' experiences. The story I heard many times over from those who had lived in Silesia was that the farmers and homeowners had been asked by Russian officials to come to the market place for an important meeting. When they got there they were herded to the train station and were taken away. All they had with them were the clothes on their backs. They lost everything: their belongings, their homes, and their farms.

In contrast to the destitute refugees, we also had a well-known composer living in our midst. Wiga Gabriel was living in the *Gasthaus* in Oberholsten. He came in 1949. He was most known for writing "In München steht ein Hofbräuhaus," a famous drinking song, but had written many other hits before the war. The Gasthaus had a piano that he used for his work. He also wrote reviews and articles for newspapers. One evening, when we took Trudel, who was visiting, to have a drink at the Gasthaus bar, she recognized him. We introduced ourselves, began a friendly conversation, and sat with him, enjoying a beer. Günter developed a friendship with him, and they sat together whenever Günter had the chance to go there for a beer. One time, Wiga told him how he had written "In München steht ein Hofbräuhaus" while sitting in a cafe in Berlin. He had done this for a friend who had written the lyrics. Wiga also helped arrange the music for the *Männerchor*, the men's choir. Sometime later he married a very nice young lady, Emmi, and they bought a farmer's cottage and remodeled it. We visited them there a number of times and always had an enjoyable time. As economic times gradually improved, he was often away, traveling on business.

One time, several members of the singing club decided to perform a play. It was about a rich landowner who had to call in the police because a poor farmer had cut down a small Christmas tree on his property. Günter played the part of the police officer. He dug out his old army uniform and high boots for his costume. The group practiced several times a week in the evenings and also built a small stage in the hall of the Gasthaus. Rows of benches filled the rest of the hall. The children sat on the front benches to watch the play. The plot contained many exciting moments, like when the landowner caught the poor farmer cutting the tree, or when the policeman suddenly appeared. And who jumped up with excitement when these parts came? Bernd! He was extremely wrapped up in the story. Others cried at the sad parts. The play was such a success that they had to add two extra performances. These types of events really brought the local people and the refugee community together.

Oberholsten was in the British Occupation Zone. Not far from Oberholsten, near Oldendorf, a small castle that had belonged to a baron was being occupied by General Montgomery as his headquarters. At times when we were on the road to Oldendorf on our bicycles, we would meet a procession of motorcycles surrounding a car carrying the general. I saw him several times through the car windows: he was heavily guarded.

The British soldiers were told not to fraternize with the German population. Many times the children ran to the side of the road to wave because they saw that a soldier was coming down the road on his horse. The mothers were there as well. But the British soldiers rode by on their horses, noses up in the air, acting as if we weren't even there. This was a dramatic change from the friendly American soldiers that we had encountered in Gröningen. There were some, though, who ventured into the villages and struck up friendships. They were not being fed well and would barter tea, coffee, or chocolate for potatoes or a sausage — something that would stick to their ribs.

One afternoon, we were working in the Schnittger's potato field when we noticed a jeep had stopped by the roadside. Two soldiers got out and walked toward us. They couldn't speak German, and the only one who could speak a little English was me. They wanted to trade coffee for potatoes. I was able to converse with them a little, and they seemed to enjoy the friendly back and forth. Shortly afterwards, they came by again. This time Günter and Trudel, who was visiting again, were also there, and we all enjoyed trying to talk to each other. They stopped by often after that. I believe they missed their families. One in particular loved Bernd. Whenever that soldier came our way and Bernd was outside he gave Bernd chocolate, held him and talked to him, or took his little hand

and walked around with him. Several times they accepted our invitation to play Rummy with us in the evening. They said that they really liked Germany and admitted that the rations given them by their army left them hungry. It made us realize that not only were Germans suffering, but so were the common people in Great Britain.

One Sunday afternoon, I was washing the dishes. Bernd was taking his nap, and Günter and my mother were taking a walk. I heard knocking on the door, and when I opened it, there stood our two British friends. They had come to say good-bye because they had gotten sudden orders to leave. They could only stay for a short while, unfortunately not long enough for the others to come back from their walk. But while they were talking to me one grabbed a towel and helped with the dishes! When they left I was happy for them because they were going to be reunited with their families soon.

Our life, generally, seemed somewhat primitive, and we had to work hard, but we were resourceful and made the best of what we had. I had to wear the same dress for a week, but kept myself looking nice by wearing clean, pressed aprons over the dress, changing them when necessary. Bernd and the other small children wore hand-knit sweaters, leggings, and socks that were made from unraveled wool from handed-down adult clothing or from the wool of the few sheep that the Fritgens owned. After shearing, they sent the wool to a place that cleaned it and spun it into yarn. We had another advantage over other refugees. Both Elisabeth and Trudel sent us clothing. Elisabeth had a talent of taking apart old clothing and sewing it into a new garment. Trudel was working for our uncle, whose business at the time was to sew uniforms for American soldiers. Often there were enough big pieces of fabric left over to make pants for Bernd and Günter. Trudel also sent extra cloth from which *Frau* Nickisch sewed items for us.

We made our homes as nice as possible. There was always a clean, white tablecloth on the table, as was the custom, and a fresh bouquet of flowers whenever possible. Hand-stitched pillows decorated our couch, and the windows had curtains.

I used the Fritgen's large laundry kettle to do my laundry. The process went like this: first, the dirty laundry soaked for a while in a pre-soak solution in a large kettle and then was rinsed in a tub filled with clean water. Then the laundry was placed back into the kettle that had been filled with clean, soapy water and brought to a boil on the big wood-burning stove that sat in the outside entryway. It was then rinsed again. I washed laundry every two or three weeks because others needed to use the kettle, not only for laundry but for mixing up food for the pigs. After the washing process, the clothes were hung on the clothesline to dry. Drying the laundry in the fall was a problem. This part of Germany had many days of dense fog in the fall months. Sometimes the damp laundry hung there for days. Except for draping a few wet items over the backs of chairs, I had nowhere inside the house to hang laundry. Then came the ironing. I used an old, heavy iron that first had to be heated on the stove, and then I held it with a pot holder to do the ironing. This was especially uncomfortable on hot summer days because I first had to build a fire for the stove top to become hot enough to heat the iron. And it seemed that everything needed to be ironed, not just our clothes but also the

tablecloths and napkins that we always used. I even ironed
diapers to disinfect them. Since I had to wash diapers more
frequently, after soaking them, I rinsed them and washed
them outside at the pump. This was very uncomfortable in
the cold winter months. Then I put them in a pot with soap
and boiled them on the stove, after which they were rinsed
again and dried.

The lack of a telephone and a car also made life a
challenge. If an important call needed to be made we could
do so from the mayor's office, but for transportation, all
that we had were our bicycles. A blister on my index finger
caused by peeling so many pears during canning time had
become infected. It was very painful and throbbing. A red
line, indicating blood poisoning, was already visible on
my lower arm, and I knew it was time to go to the doctor.
When I called the doctor in Oldendorf, I was told that he
wasn't in, and that I should go to Melle (six miles away) to a
surgeon who practiced there. So I put my aching hand into
a sling and, one handed, rode my bike clear to Melle. The
trip included several hills. The surgeon had an opening and
was able to take me immediately. He anesthetized me, cut
out the infection, and bandaged the entire hand. At first
after waking up I was woozy and felt nauseous and had to
lay down on a couch in a nearby room for a while. When I
felt a little better I got back on my bike and once again rode
one-handed back to Oberholsten, often having to push the
bike up the hills.

Despite the hardships we had to endure, we considered
ourselves fortunate. Right after the war ended, many people
in the cities were starving, whereas we had good country
food to nourish us. We lived in a pleasant area surrounded by

pleasant people, and more and more products were becoming available to us in our small country store, whereas people in the cities were still waiting in long lines, often to find that what they were waiting to buy was already sold out.

Meat was not plentiful, but we raised a pig and also invested in rabbits. The rabbits proved to be an excellent investment because they reproduced so frequently. We placed the adult rabbits in cages by themselves and fed them discarded greens from the garden and dandelion greens that we picked along the fence rows between the fields until they got big and meaty. When the time came, *Herr* Fritgen butchered the rabbits for us and kept the fur to sell. A nice, fat rabbit provided for a delicious Sunday dinner.

The pig was a little more work. Every day, I had to boil potatoes, mash them, then mix them with whatever grains we could get — oats, rye, or wheat — and feed that to the pig to fatten it up. When it came time to butcher, the farmers got together to help each other. A government inspector had to be there to check for trichinosis. A portion of the meat had to be given to the government as part of the rationing process. Because our pig was feeding a family of four (including my father-in-law), we were allowed to keep most of it. We salted some of the meat, dried some of it, made sausage and blood pudding with some of it, and canned the rest.

Mushrooms often substituted for meat. There were spring and fall mushrooms growing in the woods. Günter's father often picked for us. Sometimes in the fall, when Müller was on a business trip, my mother, on her way to visit us, took the long way through the woods, picked a pocketful of mushrooms, and then we fried them for our meal. Those we didn't fry were washed, threaded with a string, and hung over the stove to dry for winter use.

Also in the fall, *Heidlbeeren*, small, very tasty blueberries, grew on low bushes in the woods. I often got up early, around five o'clock, to pick the *Heidelbeeren* before the children woke up. The only downside was that the mosquitoes were abundant in the woods at this time and almost ate me up. We had no repellant. The berries added to the fruits we got from the apple, cherry, and pear trees in the large orchard. The apples and pears lasted most of the winter. We canned the cherries.

We also harvested many vegetables from the garden. We did have one problem: wild hogs. They were big and mean and foraged through the gardens, ruining many of the plants. We couldn't shoot them because Germans weren't allowed to have guns. There were officials for hire that would come and shoot them, but that was an added expense.

In March, I realized I was pregnant again. Günter and I wanted to take a little vacation before my pregnancy became too advanced. My father-in-law could stay with Bernd, so we planned our trip. I wanted Günter to see where I was born and to meet my relatives in Schmölz.

Eager to see everyone again, we took the train to Kronach and booked a room for two nights at a hotel. My cousin Lotte lived there, so we visited her before we walked the five miles southwest to Schmölz. When we arrived, I saw that the area had not been affected by the war. Fortunately for the residents, it was such a small, insignificant village that it was ignored. The grist mill, which my uncle owned and which had seemed so romantic when I was young and had visited them, was no longer in use and was in disrepair. I remembered standing on a raft that my uncle had made for me, pushing it around the small pond adjacent to the mill on a summer day. However, the pond was no longer filled with water, and the whole area looked poorer than I had remembered.

Our first stop when we arrived in the village was the home of my aunt and uncle, *Onkel* Schorsch and *Tante* Liena. *Onkel* Schorsch had made it back safely from the war and had continued to work in his small tailor shop. He was considered a master tailor, a talent that ran through that side of the family. Their daughter, Leni, also had this talent. She could pick out a dress in a catalogue and make that exact dress. During our visit, he told us that he had also been interned by the Americans, but his experience was good. He earned privileges because he tailored uniforms for the American officers. There was also a dentist at the camp who provided him with a new set of false teeth, a luxury that he had not been able to afford before the war.

We also visited my *Tante* Rettel and then walked back to our hotel. The next day we walked to Unterrodach, a village five miles northeast of Kronach, to visit *Tante* Schulli and her daughter, Hilde. During that visit, she told me that we had a relative in the United States, that they corresponded, and that she periodically received packages from her. She said, "Leni, why don't you also write to her? You know some English."

I liked the idea, so she asked Hilde to get the address for me. Hilde acted very oddly and said that she didn't know where the address was. She probably thought that she would get less sent to her if I was also corresponding. So *Tante* Schulli had to give it to me from memory. The relative's name was Kathryn Fisher. The street was Sandusky Street. She couldn't remember the spelling of the town, so we spelled it Bukirus. The state was Ohio (The town was actually Bucyrus. Luckily, my first letter made it despite the incorrect spelling).

Tante Schulli then also said, "Do you know that your father is living here in Unterrodach? I told him that you were coming here for a visit, and he would like for you to visit him, too." I had no idea where he had been living and had heard nothing from him since the war ended. My mother and sisters hadn't wanted anything to do with him. But my thoughts were that he had worked hard to provide well for us, and if he and my mother had their problems, usually there were faults on both sides, and I shouldn't damn him forever for leaving her. So we decided to visit him that afternoon.

My father lived in an apartment that was on the third floor of the local school building. As we walked to the building, I was very apprehensive. I thought of how very strict he was when I was growing up and how he didn't seem to have patience for us children because he was focused on building his business. Also, I had been a teenager, involved with my own activities, when he left for the war and hadn't been very close to him. Then I married without his permission. I also carried some anger because he had divorced my mother and married another woman. My heart was pounding. When he opened the house door to my knock, he just stood there, showing such happiness, and tears streamed down his face. We hugged, and I, too, began to cry. All of my apprehension melted away. He shook Günter's hand and apologized for not giving us the permission to marry. I could see that our relationship was no longer father to child, but a respectful relationship of father to grown daughter. Then he introduced his wife, Maria, their four-year-old daughter, Doris, and their baby boy, Bernhard. I had no preconceived ideas of his new family and held no grudges toward them. The wife was very nice to me and politely stayed in the background so that we could enjoy our family reunion. She had baked a cake, and we sat and talked while we ate our cake and drank coffee. My father wanted to know all about our lives and said that he regretted that Trudel and Elisabeth didn't want to have anything to do with him. He also asked about my mother and continued to do so in subsequent letters. He had very little money. He had lost everything in the war and was working as a waiter. Later they moved to Düsseldorf, where he again bought and ran a restaurant. We spent the afternoon with him, and when it was time to walk back to Kronach, he offered to accompany us with his bicycle which he could then ride back. He took us all the way back to our hotel, conversing with Günter about the war and the future of Germany. At the hotel Günter invited him up to our room for a beer and more conversation, which he accepted. When it was beginning to get dark he said that he had better start back for home. We agreed to write to each other, and we extended an invitation that he visit us in Oberholsten. After he left I was so glad that I had not been stubborn about meeting with him. It had been such a nice reunion.

⁓

I was not yet showing and had not told any of the relatives that I was pregnant. This time I did not have morning sickness and heartburn as I had had with Bernd. I felt fine throughout the pregnancy, except toward the end I tired more easily and could not help the farmers as I had in years past. I also had trouble lifting the heavy, wet laundry. *Frau* Nickisch helped me with the laundry, and Günter paid her.

In mid-September, two weeks before my due date, I went into labor. Günter rode his bike to the mayor's house to call the midwife to come to our house. She was a forty-year-old, chubby, motherly looking woman and drove around on a small moped. We could already hear the sputtering motor sound from a distance as she approached. While she was with me I was lying on our couch. The contractions would begin, then would stop for a time, and that pattern repeated. After a while, she determined that I was having Braxton Hicks contractions and it was not yet time to have the baby.

Two more weeks went by without incident. Then, on the morning of October 1, 1948, I began to have slight contractions. I thought, "If this is the real thing now, I at least want to have a clean kitchen." So, I got down on my hands and knees and scrubbed the kitchen and entryway floor. Günter again called the midwife, and I sent Bernd to get my mother, who was hoeing potatoes in the garden near the basement that Müller had started building, about one half mile from us. When they returned we sent Bernd to stay with the Nagels.

I stayed in our bedroom and, with Günter on one side and my mother on the other, the midwife delivered our new baby daughter. The delivery went quickly: she was only four and a half pounds. Because she was so tiny, the midwife suggested I always put a hot water bottle beside her when I laid her down. At that time no incubators were available. Because her crib seemed so large, we laid her in the baby buggy.

We named our daughter Helga. Soon word traveled from farm to farm that the Witzmanns had a baby girl. As was the norm at that time, I stayed in bed for a week, and many neighbors visited. When they heard the news, they brought gifts of food: home baked bread, eggs, and vegetables and fruits from their cellars.

At first I was a little concerned that Helga was too tiny. We carried her around on a pillow, but the doctor who came to examine her said that the little ones were usually tougher than the big fat ones! The midwife also returned several more times in that first week to make sure the baby was getting enough milk. To determine that, she weighed Helga before and after I nursed her. I did have to supplement my milk with formula.

We were now a little more crowded with two cribs in our small bedroom. Günter's father continued to sleep on the couch in our living room.

Both my mother and Günter's father helped out with Bernd in those first few weeks. When Helga was two months old, my mother-in-law was released from the Russian zone. The elderly were allowed to leave so that they would be less of a burden on the new local government. Now she was also able to enjoy her new granddaughter. We also received news that Herta had given birth to a baby girl, Cordula, on October 1, too. We always called them the twin cousins.

My in-laws were given a small room to rent in a farmhouse along a road that was located a short distance behind our farm. We could walk there by crossing over a field. They were, of course, happy to be together again, but were living in very cramped conditions. Their apartment consisted of only one room into which they had crammed two single beds, a cook stove, a table and chairs, and a cabinet. The farm was run by a very nice, older couple who gave them extra home-made bread and garden vegetables from time to time.

One afternoon, I was talking to my mother-in-law, not paying attention to Helga lying on the table next to me. I had pushed a small table to serve as a changing table near the stove, so that I had a warm place to bathe and change her. Suddenly we heard her screaming, lying on the floor. Helga had rolled over and fallen off of the table. My heart was in my throat. I was afraid that she may have received serious injuries. The doctor quickly came, examined her from top to bottom, including her eye reactions, and declared her injury free. He said that babies have such soft bones that they rarely break them at such a young age. I was so relieved!

At the end of November, we arranged to have Helga baptized in the Lutheran Church in Oldendorf because Oberholsten had no church. When we talked to the pastor to set a date he said that because we had not been married in a church, we would have to go through a short ceremony and receive God's blessing to our marriage. Our wedding had been a religious ceremony officiated by a pastor but had taken place in our restaurant. We complied and had my mother and Anna Drees there as witnesses. We had not needed this special ceremony for Bernd's baptism. We knew this pastor from his previous visits. He rode his bike through rain and wind and snow to visit the people in his parish, often bringing along religious pamphlets for us to read. He did this because people could not attend church on a regular basis. Since few had cars, it took a long time to get there. We also didn't have the proper clothes or shoes. Most of us wore wooden shoes in our daily lives and didn't feel this was proper footwear for a church service.

Elisabeth, Helga's godmother, was there for the baptism. She also brought along secondhand clothes from her daughter, Christine, who had been born in April of the previous year. The weather was terrible — cold with heavy rain — but *Herr* Fritgen said he would take us to the church in his buggy, since it could be enclosed. It took him a long time to hitch up the horse and get the buggy ready in the driving rain, so we were late getting started. Part of the baptism custom was that the midwife, who brought the child into the world, waited for the parents in front of the church, received the child into her arms, and carried it into the sanctuary. Our midwife was anxiously waiting for us, and when I handed Helga over to her she said, "We thought you weren't coming! The congregation has already sung the opening hymn three times!" When we entered the sanctuary, all stood up and we were led to sit in the front of the church. After the sermon, Elisabeth held Helga during the baptism ceremony, and afterward I took her to the altar, kneeled, and we both received a blessing. That was a nice custom. After the church service, we enjoyed a nice dinner in our little kitchen.

Both children thrived as they were growing up in the country. Although Bernd had beautiful, curly, dark blond hair, Helga had only very fine, light blonde hair that, at first, seemed like it would never grow. She was small for her age, but so quick. She learned to walk at the age of ten months, and that soon changed to running, even while wearing little wooden shoes. One day, when Helga was two years old, I was busy with my mother canning pears. Helga was playing nearby. Suddenly we noticed that she was gone. We looked in all the other rooms and around the outside of the house, calling her name, when suddenly, out the corner of my eye, I noticed her white-blonde head disappearing around a corner. She was heading for the road! I figured she wanted to go to her *Opa* and *Großmama's* (grandmother's) house. I raced after her, and as I neared the road I saw her standing quietly beside it with the Fritgen's German Shepherd directly in front of her, keeping her from moving forward. Afterward, I felt the dog had been protecting her.

Helga and the dog were pals, and she often played with him and gave him treats, usually bones from our meals. But one day the dog bit Helga. She had given him some bones, but one had fallen beside his bowl. As she picked it up the dog grabbed her arm, probably thinking she was going to take it from him. It didn't take much for the dog's teeth to puncture such a tender little arm. Helga screamed while the blood spurted from the arm. I was able to stop the bleeding quickly, bandaged it tightly, and took her on the bike to Oldendorf to have the doctor check it.

Later that year she gave me another heart-stopping scare when she fell down the open plank cellar stairway of the house we were building. It was a cold day, so she was bundled up in warm clothing, plus a warm winter coat with the hood up. She had been standing at the top of the stairs, and suddenly I heard her screaming, lying at the bottom. After close inspection, there were no broken bones, no scratches, and nothing hurt. It was the scare of falling that caused the screaming. All the clothing had served as padding as she rolled down the stairway.

The children were loved by all their grandparents. But it was their *Opa* who spent the most time with them. My mother sometimes went on trips with her husband, and

Günter's mother was more inclined to stay in the room and read or do crossword puzzles than traipse with them through the fields and woods. She did have a box of buttons, and Helga couldn't wait to climb up on a chair and play on the table with those buttons.

Bernd and Günter's father continued to have a strong relationship. On Sundays, they hunted mushrooms in the woods until they filled up a big basket. There were also big anthills in the woods and, if Günter's father saw one, he would sit down by it and stick his arm into the anthill so that he would get bitten. He said it eased his arthritis pain.

There weren't other children living close by who were Bernd's age with whom he could play, so he spent a lot of time with the farmers. He helped *Herr* Fritgen herd his ten milk cows from the barn to the fields near the woods. One day, *Herr* Fritgen let him drive the big Clydesdale work horses back to the barn by himself. Bernd was so proud of that! At times, *Herr* Nagel let Bernd sit beside him on the seat at the front of the flat bed wagon while he made his milk runs. Sometimes Bernd went into the fields to watch the farmers working. He knew all the work horses and could recognize them and the wagons they were pulling from far away. In the winter, he enjoyed sledding down the hills. He also helped at home. His job was to pick greens for the rabbits, which he gladly did.

When he started school, there was only one other pupil in Bernd's first grade class: the daughter of the refugee woman who lived in the other room of our farm house. Bernd walked the half mile to the two-room school house in Oldendorf every day in all kinds of weather. It was safe because there were seldom cars on the road. If a farmer happened to pass by, he would give Bernd a ride. At the end of his first year, the girl in his class failed, so he was the only student in the second grade.

Although Bernd was generally a very healthy boy, he did come down with the Spanish flu in October, 1950, and we had to send him to a youth camp on the North Sea for a month to recuperate and recover. The sea air worked wonders, and he came back a healthy, happy boy.

❦

Müller bought a piece of land approximately a half mile from where we were living and planned to build a big house. He built a huge basement, put a cement covering on it, and then lost interest (or sufficient money). After it sat there for a few months, Günter and I decided to buy it and build a house on it before it fell into disrepair. Günter had now mastered the mason trade, and homes there were mainly built out of stones, blocks, and bricks. We also felt it was time to move out of the two little rooms. It was getting cramped with two small children. So, we went to the bank and were approved for a loan.

Günter bought the materials and lumber to build a scaffold, and he worked on our future home in the evenings after work and on the weekends. The sand that was used for the mortar contained larger stones and had to be sifted. To do this, a mesh wire frame was set up at an angle, and the sand was scooped up with a shovel and thrown against the frame. The larger stones fell on one side and the fine sand went through the mesh. This was hard work. My mother often came to help me with this job. We took turns. When one of us was exhausted, the other took over. Then we mixed the filtered sand and cement together in a large tub, added water, and took the mortar to Günter. This was also exhausting because the buckets were very heavy, and the house was two stories high. The outside walls were double-layered: an inner wall of concrete blocks, a small space that insulated, and an outer wall of bricks. One afternoon, Günter was up on the scaffolding when it suddenly began to move back and forth. It was a little scary, but then it abated. We later heard that there had been a small earthquake in the area!

When the walls were finished, carpenters put up the roof, and when they were finished, it was time to have a *Richtefest*, a "finishing" party, and add the tiles to the roof (the roofs were covered with clay tiles, made of a similar material to bricks). First a large wreath with flowing, colorful ribbons was placed at the top of the roof. All the neighbors, even the wives, came to take part in this work and celebration. They formed a line and handed the tiles from where they had been unloaded from person to person until they reached the men who were on the roof. This was the traditional way to finish a house, and all of us had fun working together. I had made sandwiches, and we offered beer and Schnapps. There was a party atmosphere, and in no time the roof was finished.

The house was built over half of the original basement because it would have otherwise been way too large. The other half was going to serve as a patio. We also did not finish the first floor, rather just the second floor. Our aim was to live in the second floor while finishing the first floor and then rent it out to earn money to pay our loan and make further improvements. Our second-floor home consisted of a living room/kitchen area and a bedroom. All four of us slept in the bedroom. Bernd had small bed, Helga slept in a crib, and Günter and I slept on two couches that my mother had given us. The double bed in the farm house had belonged to the Fritgens. An open, wooden, plank stairway led to this first floor. There was also a bathroom, but at first, we had no running water, so I had to lug all of our water from the well and up those stairs. We also had no electricity yet because no new electric lines were available at that time in our area. Many farmers still had their old oil lamps from before the time when they had first installed electricity, and the Nagels lent us one of theirs. It was a beautiful cut glass lamp. We hung it in the main room. I had to clean the glass every day from the soot that accumulated on it. We also had a flashlight and a radio, both of which ran on batteries. To recharge the radio battery, we had to take it to a place in Oldendorf. It seemed like the battery would always wear out right during a suspenseful moment in one of the programs that had captured our attention!

Life, although challenging, was dotted with good times. Various school friends of Günter who had survived the war visited us. Sundays, a few weekday evenings, and holidays also offered us brief respite from our work.

Christmases in Oberholsten were joyous times. We gathered pine branches to make a small wreath which we set in the middle of our table. We placed four red candles on the wreath to light on the Advent Sundays. Each Sunday one more candle was lit until all four were burning brightly. The excitement for the children was that Christmas Eve would soon follow. On the eve of St. Nikolas Day, Bernd and Helga put their shoes outside the door in hopes that St. Nikolas would fill them with goodies while they were sleeping. In the morning, they would find them filled with candies.

The farmers who owned woods didn't mind if we cut a small pine tree, so Günter would cut a fresh tree the morning of the 24th, and we would decorate it with glass blown Christmas bulbs that he had bought through the black market and with tinsel we were able to buy in the stores. Small, slender candles were then clipped to the ends of the branches. They were lit for the first time on Christmas Eve. The combination of the smell of the burning candles combined with the fresh pine smell was wonderful! I always baked a *Stolle*, which was a special Christmas bread, and cookies. On Christmas Eve, we distracted the children while the *Weihnachtsmann* came and put toys under the tree. Then we sang Christmas carols, enjoyed our gifts and treats, and read Christmas poems and stories. We couldn't go to a Christmas Eve church service because we would have had to walk one and a half miles to the church in Oldendorf. It was just too far on those cold December nights with the children.

In Germany, there are two official Christmas holidays. On the first day of the Christmas holiday, our parents joined us, and we exchanged small presents. My mother-in-law always saw to it that the children were given books. They loved hearing the stories from those children's books over and over. We would have a nice dinner, followed by games, and then they would have to walk back to their homes before darkness set in. We rested and enjoyed playing with the children on the second Christmas Day.

At Easter time, Bernd and Helga collected moss from the base of the trees at the edge of the woods. With the moss, they built small nests in a secluded spot in the yard in which the Easter Bunny could deposit the eggs and candies. Besides finding the goodies on Easter morning, they hunted the colored eggs which were hidden around the yard and in the bushes. Easter Day included a special dinner (we butchered one of our rabbits for the occasion) with our parents. Easter was also a two-day holiday, so we again enjoyed an extra day of rest and relaxation. If the weather was nice, we took Bernd and Helga on a bicycle ride. Günter wound cloth strips around his handle bars so Bernd could sit on them comfortably. I had a basket in front of my handlebars where Helga sat.

On warm evenings during spring through fall, before the children's bedtime, we often took leisurely walks into the woods and hunted mushrooms. The surrounding woods were part of the Oldendorf's castle estate. The forest rangers in their dark green uniforms kept them very tidy; any fallen branches had been removed for firewood and any sick trees were felled before they could topple on their own and cause damage to the healthy trees. We could see far into the woods, and the smell was fresh and clean.

I also often walked into the woods to collect branches, which the owners of the castle allowed the people to do. One morning, with Bernd and Helga walking by my side, I pulled a small wagon to the place where I normally found nice branches. However, on this day, there weren't many to be found. I did see a small tree that looked dried out and dead, but had not yet fallen. I was able to knock it over. Just as the tree was falling, a ranger approached me! I was afraid that I was going to get into trouble, but he was friendly. He asked me if I was looking for firewood, and I replied that yes, I was only taking what was dry. He smiled and told me that was fine, but I was to make sure that I didn't chop down any trees! I felt lucky that he was so nice about it. Another ranger, who might have been impressed with himself in his uniform and eager to use his authority, might have given me a tongue lashing and fined me.

At age twenty-eight I noticed that my vision was beginning to fail. My eyes would quickly tire when I was darning or doing any other kind of hand stitching. I had to go all the way to Melle to see the eye doctor. He diagnosed me as being neither far nor near-sighted, but having a condition in which the nerves would not let me focus clearly, causing my eyes to tire. So I began wearing glasses, but only for reading and close-up work. Otherwise, I didn't need them.

9

THE EMIGRATION
PROCESS

MAY 1950 - OCTOBER 1952

I n 1952 large numbers of Germans were emigrating to
Canada, South America, and the United States. When they
got through their workday, they had just enough money to
cover the cost of food and nothing else. Many could no longer
envision a future in Europe and were also afraid of further
Soviet aggression.

❦

By now I had established a regular correspondence with
Kathryn Fisher, although there was a four to six week wait
between letters. She had also sent some care packages with
clothes for me and the children. I learned many interesting
things from her letters. Her husband, Dr. Lester L. Fisher,
was a dentist, and she had one daughter, Sharon. I began to
remember some of the English I had learned in school, but
my father-in-law helped me write the letters. I would write
them in German, he would translate them into English,
and I would copy the English into my own handwriting. He
also helped me read Kathryn's letters. In one of my letters, I

mentioned that the prospects in Germany seemed bleak. I explained that Günter was working in construction and that we had read that German construction workers were being sought after in South America, so we were considering going there. In her next letter, Kathryn said that we should come to the United States, and that she would sponsor us. She said that her grandparents' house in New Washington, Ohio, stood empty, and that they would fix it up for us to live in. They could help us.

That was quite a bit of news for us to digest. Günter and I discussed it at length. Could we leave our aging parents here in Germany? When we talked it over with our parents, they heartily encouraged us to go. They, too, agreed that the future in Germany looked bleak. It seemed impossible to get ahead financially. Both of our savings were stuck in banks in the Russian zone, and we knew that we would never see that money. We were also politically fearful. The United States had not interfered during the communist aggression of China and were slow to react in Korea. If the American troops should lose the war in Korea, we feared that the Allied occupying forces in Germany would be too weak to resist an aggression from the east, and our lot would be sealed. Finally, we decided that it would be a good opportunity for us.

In the late spring of 1950, we contacted the U.S. embassy in Bremen to see what steps we needed to take to emigrate. They sent us documents, which we filled out, and in early July, we received our emigration number. The number of emigrants to the United States in a year's time was limited, so we knew that our number might not be called until the following year. We continued to live as though this was only a dream that may or may not come true. Günter continued to pedal his bicycle to distant construction sites, he continued to work on our house, and I planted our garden.

We thought that the process was running smoothly, but then on January 26, 1951, we were suddenly notified by mail that our number had been deleted, and we could not emigrate because both Günter and I had been members of the Hitler Youth! We were stunned. At that time we were only teenagers and didn't totally understand the ramifications of being part of that organization. All young people had automatically been a part of it. We immediately wrote to Kathryn. She wrote to the embassy herself and tried to help, but to no avail.

Six months later, we were again contacted by the embassy and told that the law had been changed and that people who were in the Hitler Youth were no longer considered dangerous for simply having been members. We had to complete the entire paperwork process again, starting from scratch, as did the Fishers. But we were successful and were given a new number!

In April of 1952, we received a letter to come to Bremen. We borrowed a car and, with the children, drove to the embassy. After registering, we sat in a waiting room, appropriately named because we waited for a long time until we were finally called to an office where we answered many different questions. Günter was grilled about his membership in the Nazi party. He explained to the U.S. official that he had been drafted into the army but had never signed anything to join the party. He had been automatically conscripted into the party without his knowledge. They accepted his explanation, which was the truth. Then we had to swear an oath that all of the information we gave was truthful. We were amazed that, even with all the destruction during the war, they still had papers showing all of the party members. After that, we waited again in the waiting room until we were called for our physical examinations. Even the children were examined. Mainly, they checked for infectious diseases and X-rayed our lungs; they were screening for tuberculosis. We weren't worried about the exam because we knew we were in good health. Again we sat waiting, this time for the results. Finally, a nurse came out and walked over to me with my X-ray. She said that there was a shadow on one of my lungs. This could have been due to an ineffective X-ray, or I might have had lung cancer. So I followed her back in to have a second X-ray taken. While waiting for those results, my worried thoughts passed through all kinds of scenarios of what would be if they found that I had cancer. After a short time, the nurse called me back in and told me that all was in order. What a relief!

We left the building weary but happy that all had gone well. The fee amounted to 150 DM, a whole month's unemployment pay that Günter had been receiving for the cold months when no construction had taken place. We had borrowed this amount in advance and planned to pay it off gradually now that construction had begun again after the long winter months. In a few months, we would be able to finalize the paperwork with the consulate, and we could get our visas. These, too, cost a lot of money — 37.80 DM for each person. We had asked the Fishers to lend us the money for these, and we would pay them back at a later time. The day had been quite an ordeal. I was glad that the children had been well behaved.

It was already the end of May, and we had not received our visas. When Günter inquired at the consulate, he was told that there was still a problem because he had been a member of the Nazi party. He again gave them the facts and told them that he had sworn under oath to the truthfulness of his information. He was told that he would have to put the information in writing, confirming his prior statements, swear another oath before a notary, and send it to the consulate.

Six weeks later, the American consulate wanted evidence from a former acquaintance who would be able to confirm Günter's statements. He immediately wrote to some of his friends, but we were worried that they may not receive the letters. I also wrote to Kathryn because I thought a letter from her to the consulate would help. We were so disappointed with this delay. By now we had set our hearts on emigrating into the United States.

On Tuesday afternoon, August 19, we got a telegram from the consul general asking us to appear at the consulate on Thursday morning at nine o'clock for a re-examination of our visa situation. This time all went smoothly, and we left the consulate with our visas.

In mid-September, we were summoned to Bremen again to pick up our finalized paperwork. Günter and I took the train this time and walked to the embassy building. Our paperwork was ready and waiting for us. Our next step was to book passage on an ocean liner, so we walked to the nearest travel agency. We were told that so many emigrants were leaving the country that most ships had a seven to eight month waiting period. We were dismayed at this information, but had hopes that other agencies could help us. We walked to three more agencies and were told the same story. We felt so discouraged. Our papers were only valid for six months. We would have to reapply and go through the whole process again if we could not find passage within that time period.

The alternative was to ask Kathryn for a loan to fly, but that would be a big financial burden for us, both for the tickets and to ship our large trunks with our household goods separately.

We felt very disheartened at this point and were walking back to the train station when we passed another travel agency. I wanted to go in to see if they had any possibilities. Günter had lost hope that we would find something and wanted to go on, but we did go in. Inside we had to sit and wait a short time for someone to help us. While we were waiting, we heard a telephone ring, and the agent answered. When she was finished, she asked how she could help us, and we told her that we were looking for passage to New York. She asked, "For how many?" We said, "Four people." She replied, "You are in luck. I was just on the phone and it was a cancellation for four people, passage to New York."

We could hardly believe our good luck! I told Günter that this was like a gift sent from God. But, it was true. The ship, a Greek ocean liner named the TSS Neptunia, would sail on October 15 and arrive in New York on October 25. We had four weeks to sell our house and pack up what we were going to take with us.

After our passage on the TSS Neptunia was confirmed we began telling our friends and neighbors that we were emigrating to the United States. Our families, of course, had been kept abreast of our plans and setbacks over the past two years. Everyone was very happy for us, and several small celebrations were held in our honor in Oberholsten.

Our house sold quickly, a god-send, for we needed the money to help finance our trip and pay off the bank loan. We had only lived in it a year.

We realized that most of our clothes were worn-out work clothes that had been mended several times over. We didn't have the proper clothes to travel on an ocean liner to the United States. So Günter's father called for a taxi from Melle, a big black car, to pick us all up (Günter's parents and the four of us) and take us to Osnabrück to go shopping. The children were so excited to be able to ride in a car, a rare occurrence for them. We bought three large, brown, hard-leather suitcases, beige trench coats for Günter and me, dark green Loden coats with hoods for Bernd and Helga, a new suit and shirts for Günter, new underwear for everyone, and a few other needed items. I also picked out a pullover sweater for myself and Günter thought it looked so pretty that he bought me a beautiful brooch to wear with it. The money from the sale of our house helped finance our shopping spree. What a fun day that was!

Shortly after that trip, Günter's parents moved to Sontheim and were receiving a small pension. Herta and Siegfried were living in nearby Heidenheim and had found a small apartment for them. We were very happy about that because we hated to see them stuck in the rural, remote farmland near Oberholsten by themselves.

I then began packing, which required a lot of thinking about what to take along and what to give away. In a big trunk and two large wooden boxes, I packed linens that Trudel and my mother had given me, along with my dishes, cutlery, remembrances (gifts, pictures, books, jewelry), duvets, toys, and Christmas decorations. My mother also sent along a Rosenthal vase that she had saved from the restaurant for Kathryn. We really didn't have much, so one trunk and two wooden boxes were sufficient. I packed all of our clothes into the new suitcases. Our parents picked the furniture, pots and pans, and other household items they wanted, and we sold the few furniture items that were left.

❦

We had two and a half weeks left to visit our siblings and their families to say goodbye. *Herr* Müller was traveling around, teaching business classes. My mother had made plans to go with him, so we had to say our goodbyes before she left. Although it was a tearful farewell, we consoled ourselves with the fact that America was not that far away, and once we all got back on our feet financially, we would make trips to see each other.

Our first visit was by train to Bad Meinberg, a small spa city where Elisabeth had settled with Hans Max. They both worked in the small women's lingerie store which Hans Max's parents owned. They lived with their two daughters, five-year-old Christine and eight-month-old Inge, in the second-floor apartment of the in-laws' big house. It was only an overnight stay because they had to work in the store every day. Then we took the train to Bad Godesberg, on the Rhine River, where Trudel was working in the U.S. embassy.

Trudel lived in a very small apartment, so she had made arrangements for us to sleep in the guest room of the larger apartment of one of her working colleagues. Again, it was only a two-day visit because Trudel also had to work. We picked her up each day at her office and took pleasant walks along the Rhine or along the city streets and then enjoyed dinner together in a neighborhood restaurant.

Our last destination was Heidenheim to see Herta and Siegfried and Günter's parents for twelve days. We stayed with Herta and Siegfried in their small apartment, and Günter's parents came during the day. On October 1, Cordula's and Helga's fourth birthday, Herta baked a special cake and made lanterns for the children so they could participate in the lantern festival that evening. This was a festival where children formed a parade with their lit lanterns and sang songs as they walked through the neighborhood streets.

Unfortunately, Helga was sick with a sore throat and a high fever. Instead of enjoying the lantern parade, she laid in bed while I put cold compresses on her legs to try to get the fever down. She quickly rebounded and was well again within a few days. Although Siegfried had to go to work, the rest of us often took walks together, played board games, and sang old favorite songs with the accompaniment of their piano. It was an enjoyable twelve days, but then the time came for us to say our tearful goodbyes and take the train to Bremen.

<hr />

We were required to be in Bremen the day before the departure date to make sure all our papers were in order. A hotel room was included in our fare. The hotel was filled with people traveling on the Neptunia, and we enjoyed the evening talking to others making the trip. The next morning a bus took us all to Bremen's port, Bremerhaven, where the ship was anchored.

To board the ship, we moved with the throng of people from a building we had first entered, through a hallway, and directly into a large room. The room looked like a hotel lobby with hallways entering from the sides and a large, ornate carpeted stairway leading to an upper floor. We had given up the trunk and boxes for shipment, but had kept our suitcases with us. Helga kept asking, "When are we going to get on the ship?" She couldn't believe that we were already "in" the ship. She thought that we were still in a building. Because we were traveling tourist class (the cheapest fare), we entered the narrow but brightly lit hallway that led down to our cabin. We were in the bowels of the ship, and we could hear the drone of the motors from our room. Our small room had narrow bunk beds on each side with a cabinet of drawers separating them. We could hang up some clothes in two small closets at the ends of the beds and push the suitcases under the bottom bunks. The toilet and shower were down the hallway and up a set of stairs. Long, metal bars to hold onto for balance were located on the hallway walls and in the stairway.

After we had settled in, we went back up to the deck to watch our departure. It was crowded, but we found a spot along the outside railing, looking down at the pier. The atmosphere was festive. A photographer was taking pictures of those at the railing from the pier. A brass band was playing "Muss i' denn" and many were throwing streamers into the water as others were cheering. Tears were streaming down my face. I was sad to be leaving my friends, family, and country. Would we see our aging parents again? I was suddenly very afraid. From her letters, Kathryn seemed like a very nice lady, but would she really like us? And the people we would be meeting, would they be angry with us? Would they treat us with disdain? After all, our country had been at war with the U.S., and they had lost many of their fathers, sons, and brothers. My English wasn't very good. Would I be laughed at for my foreign ways? I don't know what was going through Günter's mind, but the children thought the whole thing was a great adventure. They had many questions as the ship began moving out to sea. This helped distract me from my thoughts and took my mind off of my worries.

The trip then started feeling like a grand cruise vacation. The food was wonderful. Each meal served in the big dining hall was fresh and tasty. The sea in the English Channel was calm, and the weather was sunny and warm enough to sit out on the deck. Bernd and Helga enjoyed playing in a big playroom that had all kinds of toys and even several swings. In the evenings, after the children had fallen asleep, we would go to see a movie, go dancing, or just sit in the "smoking room" and enjoy a drink or play cards.

Our first stop after we left Bremerhaven was Southhampton, England, to pick up more passengers, and after that we stopped at Cherbourg, France and Cork, Ireland. Most of the Irish who boarded in Cork stayed in the tourist class rooms near ours. At night, when we wanted to sleep, they gathered in the hallway and sang Irish songs and danced. At first it was entertaining, but after a few nights it became irritating. But we had to admit that they were a fun-loving group.

As soon as we left Cork and entered the open ocean, the high waves pulled the ship up and down and rocked it from side to side. I became seriously sea sick. I tried taking pills that the ship's doctor had given me, but they didn't help. I was not able to eat in the dining room anymore and lived on crackers and tea in my bunk. At times the weather was warm enough so that I could bundle up in my coat and lie on a deck chair to take in the fresh sea air. But to get from our room to the deck, I had to pass the dining room and smell the aromas from the kitchen. This always set me off. I had to run the rest of the way to the deck and would arrive just in time to throw up over the railing.

There was only one vicious storm during our crossing, near Halifax, Canada. One wall of the smoking room was smashed in and all the tables and chairs ended up in a big pile in an inner corner. We couldn't walk down the hallways without being knocked from one side to the other. The only way to make progress was to use the bars to pull ourselves forward. Once we left Halifax, the waters along the coast were calm, and the seasickness disappeared. From Halifax to New York City, I was once again able to enjoy the trip.

When we arrived in New York on Tuesday, October 28, it was already dark, and the ship was not allowed to enter the harbor. The trip took twelve days instead of the predicted ten because of the storm. From where our ship was anchored, we could see the brightly lit Statue of Liberty and all of the lights of the skyscrapers in the city. We also saw the lights of the heavy traffic on the street that bordered the harbor. What a sight that was for us! Its impression on me was indescribable. The thought that we had almost achieved the end of our journey was comforting.

But then all of my doubts began creeping back into my thoughts again, and I spent the night awake. I worried that we would not find the Fishers, especially since we were two days delayed, or that my English would not be good enough to communicate with them. I had continued to practice English with my father-in-law and had bought English magazines to practice reading.

The next morning we had to be ready to leave the ship by 6:00 a.m. I had packed most of our luggage items the night before. When we began to feel the movement of the ship, we knew we had to get ready quickly, pack our few remaining things, and rush up to the dining hall to grab a quick breakfast. The ship did not take long to ease into the Hoboken harbor and dock. We grabbed our suitcases and went to the deck to stand in line for a long time for customs inspection. From where we were standing, we could see people waiting on the pier. Kathryn had written that she would be wearing a long, black coat and a green hat, and that she was heavy. There was a family of three, and the woman fit her description. We had also exchanged pictures to help us recognize each other. I asked Günter to go closer to the railing and wave to them. I was shy about doing that myself, and he was taller and could be seen better. They saw him and waved back to him. I felt better knowing they knew we were there.

Suddenly, we heard on the loudspeaker that families with children could go through first, which we did. We were taken immediately, and since our papers were all in order, we went quickly through the process. We proceeded down the stairway to the pier to where the Fishers were waiting. Kathryn immediately took me in her arms. She then introduced us to her husband, Doc, and thirteen-year-old daughter, Sherry. They were all so nice, and I immediately felt comfortable with them.

It was a cold, blustery October day. We all had been standing in the cold, waiting for several hours, and were chilled through and through. We hoped that the building where our trunk and boxes were to be delivered would be warmer. But as we walked into the large hall it was also cold and drafty. The children were also getting hungry. So Doc took Bernd with him, and they found a hot dog stand. They came back carrying a pile of hot dogs in buns, which satisfied everyone's hunger. We soon found the trunk under a sign marked "W." Our boxes should have been there, too, but they were nowhere in sight. We waited a while longer and, when it became evident that nothing more would be delivered, we began to worry. After a while and because we were all shivering with cold, I said I would walk around to look for the boxes. As I was walking, inspecting everything marked with a "W", I got the bright idea that maybe they had gotten turned around and were with the "M"s. Surely enough, there they were! A porter took the trunk and boxes to the B&O Railway office. From there, they were sent to our new home in New Washington. With that taken care of, we could get into the warm car and start our drive to Ohio.

The Fisher's car was a large Packard. Doc, Bernd, and Kathryn sat in the front seat. Sherry, Günter (with Helga on his lap), and I sat in the back seat. The car had a trunk large enough for our luggage. Sherry, who had a mouth full of braces, tried to make conversation with me, but I, for the life of me, could not understand anything she said. It was a little embarrassing. But Kathryn and Doc spoke clearly and also tried to use some of their minimal German. Helga was fascinated with Kathryn's felt hat because it was so soft. I had to keep telling her not to touch it. Every once in a while, unable to resist temptation, she would run her little hand across the back of the hat. Fortunately, Kathryn didn't seem to mind. Bernd sat obediently for the entire ride, taking in the new experience.

We drove until supper time and stopped at a restaurant. It was a challenge to explain to the children what the different food items were because everything on the menu was totally new to them. We finally settled on hamburgers. Helga didn't want to have anything to do with ketchup because it was too red. Already we were noticing small differences in our cultures which made our meal fun and entertaining.

We then drove a few hours longer before stopping at a roadside motel for the night. Our room had two double beds and a bathroom with a tub and shower. What a luxury! The children enjoyed the full bathtub, playing and splashing each other before settling in the bed for their first night in their new country.

The next morning, we all met for breakfast and continued our trip to Bucyrus. The plans were to live with Doc and Kathryn for a few days before we moved into the house in New Washington. When we got there we met Lewis Kibler, whom everyone called Pop. He was Kathryn's father and also lived with them. He was eager to be able to use the few German words that he knew and enjoyed telling us of his past experiences, including some Civil War stories that his father, who had served in that war, had passed along.

On Friday, we stayed at home with Kathryn, relaxed, and recovered from the trip while Doc went to his dentistry practice. It was Halloween. In the afternoon, Kathryn took me and the children to see a Halloween parade, which was a totally new experience for us. That evening, children in all kinds of costumes knocked on the house door, trick-or-treating, and Bernd and Helga had fun handing out the candies.

On Saturday, Günter and Doc went to New Washington to start up the oil stove that had been installed to heat our new home and to make sure everything was ready for us. Kathryn and Doc owned the house, and we were going to pay rent. Kathryn took me to a dress shop in town to buy me a hat. She wanted to take us to church the next day and a hat was required. I had a leather barrette that was quite fashionable in Germany, but was evidently not suitable for church. She selected a light grey pill box hat with a small netted veil in front to match my grey trench coat. I wasn't used to wearing a hat and felt comical in it.

So we began Sunday by attending Good Hope Lutheran Church in Bucyrus with the Fishers. We were asked to stand as we were introduced to the congregation, and again my apprehensions of what people thought of us welled up in me. But after the service everyone was so nice and welcoming. Many could speak a little German (most had a German background) and, with our broken English, we were able to communicate. A friend of Kathryn, Miss Louise Kibler (same name but no relation), even took us all out for Sunday dinner.

On Monday, we drove to New Washington to see our new home. It was a small, white, wood-frame house with a living room, kitchen, and small bedroom on the first floor. The second floor was a long room under the roof with a small window at each end. The only heat for this room would come from the oil stove's chimney, which passed through the middle of the room, and a register opening in the floor that allowed heat to rise from the room below. There was no running water or bathroom, just an outhouse which was a short walk from the house and an outdoor pump for the water.

I couldn't believe my eyes when I looked around. Everything we needed was there, already furnished: beds, dressers in the bedrooms, a couch and chairs in the living room, a refrigerator, a cooking stove, and a table with chairs in the kitchen. The cupboards and refrigerator were filled with food. Many people had been so kind to donate items for us.

I knew our lives would be happy here — so much kindness and opportunity awaited. The predictions of my childhood had come true. I did take a very long trip. And I had had so much good luck: surviving the illness when I was an infant, meeting Günter, having my whole family survive the war, being able to escape the Russians, finding the rooms in Oberholsten to recover from the war, and having the opportunity to come to the United States. The ringing church bells at the time of my birth that predicted my future were correct.

AFTERWORD

Helene **(Murmann) and Günter Witzmann.** Helene and Günter settled in New Washington, Ohio and became active in the community and in St. John's Lutheran Church.

Günter found employment with a local mason and worked for him for several years before starting his own masonry and plaster contractor business. In 1953, a bathroom and small living room were added to the house, and Helene and Günter bought their first car, a used Chevrolet Fleetline, for $800.

On June 6, 1954, a second son, Frank Arthur, was born. The family became naturalized citizens on November 16, 1959. Helene continued to be a homemaker and added a full-time job in 1964 with the C.E. White Company, sewing boat seat cushions.

In the mid-1960s, Günter took correspondence courses in architectural design, and in 1969, he found a job as an estimator with a construction firm in Toledo, Ohio. They bought their first house and moved to Defiance, Ohio, a small city near Toledo. Helene found a job working in the mailroom of Defiance College.

In 1977, Günter found a more challenging position as project manager with Danak, a Danish company located in New York City that built airport runways around the world. So they moved again, this time finding a small ranch house with a big yard and garden in Danbury, Connecticut.

While living there, Helene worked in the Credit and Collection Department at Grolier, Inc., receiving several promotions and awards for excellent work during her seven and a half years there. The years were filled not only with hard work, but also with enjoying their yard, vegetable garden, and fruit trees, visiting with friends and family (especially grandchildren), and traveling, including frequent trips to Germany to see old classmates and family.

Günter retired in 1985, and they moved to Danville, Ohio, where Helga was living. In the nearby countryside, with rolling hills and beautiful views, they began building Günter's German-style dream home which he had designed himself. Doing most of the work themselves and living in rooms as they were finished, bit by bit they completed the house in three years. They were able to enjoy the house, two acres of gardens, fruit and nut trees, and a wonderful view for miles until Günter received a diagnosis of pancreatic cancer. He lost his battle with the disease and died on October 16, 1998, at the age of 78. Günter had been an active Lions Club member in all of the communities in which he lived, and shortly before his death he received the Melvin Jones Fellowship Award, the highest form of recognition in that organization.

In 1997, Günter had a unique experience. He was put in contact through a social studies teacher, who interviewed World War II veterans, with a bombardier, who was part of the raid on Merseburg on May 12, 1944. Through phone calls and letters they shared their experience — the bombardier describing how he saw the train from the air and Günter describing the silvery planes high in the sky. They became friends and hoped to meet personally, but Günter's illness prevented that.

Helene moved to Bristol Village, a retirement community in Waverly, Ohio, in 2004. There she enjoyed the various activities and the company of many new friends. Helene led a very healthy life-style: swimming almost every morning for forty-five minutes in addition to walking her little terrier, Milli, for at least two miles every day. On March 5, 2014, stomach cancer took her life at the age of 89.

Bernhard Witzmann. Shortly after getting settled into the new home in New Washington, a tutor, hired by Kathryn Fisher, came for two weeks to give Bernd English lessons so that he could begin to go to school. At first the teachers thought he should be put back in the first grade. However, they saw how quickly he adapted to the English language and that his math skills were further along than his second-grade peers, so he was placed into the second grade. He quickly made friends and became known as Bernie, a name that he has used from that time on.

Bernie graduated from Buckeye Central High School and from Bluffton College with a BS in Education. He later continued his education and earned a Masters Degree in Education. He worked as a teacher and basketball coach in various schools, eventually holding the position of Athletic Director in Centerville High School near Dayton, Ohio for twenty-three years.

Since retiring in 2002 he and his wife, Pam, enjoy their lakeside home in southern Michigan and travel extensively.

Helga (Witzmann) Long. Helga quickly learned English from neighborhood children, even some swear words that her mother didn't know were "bad words," but that Kathryn Fisher quickly corrected. Helga graduated from Buckeye Central High School and from The Ohio State University with a BS in Education, also later earning her Masters Degree in Education.

She married James R. Long, a lieutenant in the U.S. Army. He was sent to Baumholder, Germany where they lived for two and a half years. During this time, Helga was able to visit with her German relatives. Their son, Daniel, was born in Bad Kreuznach and Rosa Müller was able to hold her great grandson before they returned to the States. They had two more children, daughters Kristin and Ashleigh.

Helga and Jim live near Danville, Ohio. While her children were growing up, Helga taught fitness classes in the Knox County area, then renewed her teaching certificate and taught high school German before retiring in 2015. She fills her time with gardening, staying active by walking or jogging and golfing, reading, and enjoying her eight grandchildren. Helga and Jim also like to travel and hike and hope to see most of the United States and visit Germany as well.

Frank Witzmann. After growing up in New Washington, Frank spent his last two high school years in Defiance and continued his education at Defiance College, earning a BA Degree in Natural Systems, followed with an MS Degree at Ball State University and a PhD from Marquette University, both in Biology. Frank has three children, Sarah, Katie, and Justin, and five grandchildren. He lives with his wife, Angie, near Indianapolis and is a professor of physiology at the Indiana University School of Medicine.

Rosa Müller. After the death of her husband in the mid-1950s, Rosa lived in Bad Nauheim near her brother, Adam. In 1958, she traveled to New Washington and lived with Helene and Günter for a year before moving to Darmstadt. In the late 1960's, she moved to Bad Meinberg to be with Elisabeth and Elisabeth's family until she died on September 5, 1976. She was 77 years old.

Hans Murmann. Hans continued to live in Düsseldorf with his second family. Helene stayed in touch with him and with his children. He died of lung cancer on October 8, 1967, at the age of 70.

Gertrud (Trudel) Murmann. Trudel never married; rather she followed a secretarial career. She also emigrated to the United States in 1954, lived in New York City, and worked in the garment district. She later became the personal secretary for an administrator at Columbia University. When he was offered the job of Vice President of Development at the Miami Herald, he would only accept the position if Trudi (her English nickname) would move there as well. He said that secretaries with such high qualities were hard to find. After her boss died, Trudel remained employed at the Miami Herald for a few more years but then also decided to retire. She moved to Mt. Vernon, Ohio, near Helene and Günter and near Helga and her family. Trudel died on December 18, 2005 at the age of 84.

Elisabeth (Murmann) and Hans-Max Sabokath. Elisabeth and Hans-Max continued to live in Bad Meinberg and successfully ran the store which Hans-Max had inherited from his parents. They had two daughters and a son. Elisabeth was able to see her sisters from time to time by visiting the United States or by receiving visits from them. Hans-Max died on November 16, 1997, and Elisabeth died on January 14, 1999 at the age of 76.

Artur and Gertrud Witzmann. After living in Sondheim for a few years, Artur and Gertrud found a larger apartment in Heidenheim, close to where Herta and Siegfried were living. While Artur's health was still good, in 1956, they traveled to New Washington to stay with Helene and Günter for six months. It would be the last time that Artur would see his son, daughter-in-law, and grandchildren. He died on April 25, 1957 at the age of 76 of heart failure. Gertrud continued to live in Heidenheim until her health started failing, and she moved to Dortmund, where Herta and Siegfried were now living. She died on November 16, 1969 at the age of 85.

Herta Grothendieck. Herta, with her husband, Siegfried, and children, Ekkehard and Cordula, continued to live in Heidenheim until Siegfried's job took them to Dortmund in the early 1960s. Siegfried died in the late 1980s, and Herta died on June 6, 2012 at the age of 97.

Klara and Erich Wust. Klara and Erich had two sons. Their sons were able to reach the West before the Russian Occupation Zone borders closed, but Klara and Erich were stuck in East Germany until they reached retirement age. After they were free to leave, they joined their sons in Bad Nauheim and operated a successful bakery. In August 1979, they traveled to Ohio to attend Bernie's wedding. It was the first time Klara got to see her godson since he was a baby.

Kathryn and Lester L. (Doc) Fisher. Kathryn and Doc remained close with Helene and Günter. After his retirement from the dental profession, Doc remained very active at good Hope Lutheran Church as well as in the Bucyrus community. Kathryn also stayed active in the church and in several social clubs. She died on May 3, 1982 at the age of 80, and Doc died in February 1984. He was 82 years old.

PHOTOGRAPHS

The house where Helene was born (people in the photo unknown).

Elisabeth, Helene and Trudel.

*Elisabeth, Rosa, Trudel and
Helene 1929.*

The Murnann family with neighbor girl in front of restaurant in Magdeburg.

Helene's confirmation picture, 1940.

Rosa Murmann, 1940.

The hospital in Magdeburg where Helene worked.

*In Mittenwald: unknown, Trudel, unknown, Rosa,
Elisabeth, Helene, 1941.*

*Vacation in the Black Forest, 1942;
Elisabeth, Trudel, Helene.*

Lt. Günter Paul Witzmann

Elisabeth, Rosa, Helene, and Trudel Murmann.

The wedding day, May 9, 1944.

*Herr Neuhäuser, Rosa Murmann,
Artur and Gertrud Witzmann.*

The wedding day, May 9, 1944.

— wenige Tage nach dem Luftangriff am 19. März 1945. Im Vordergrund ein Teil
zerstörten Verlagsgebäude der „Jenaischen Zeitung"

Jena: Günter's church in ruins after the March 19, 1945 bombing.

*Günter, Bernd, Herta (holding
Ekkehard), and Helene, May, 1946.*

*Günter, Bernd, and Helene,
April, 1946.*

Helga, April, 1950.

*Helga, Helene, and
Bernd, 1951.*

The house that Günter and Helene built.

*Helene, Christine, Günter, Bernd,
Elisabeth, Helga, Oct. 1952.*

Trudel, Helga, Günter, Bernd, and Helene, Oct. 1952.

*Günter, Helene, Bernd, Artur, Gertrud,
Siegfried holding Helga, Ekkehard,
and Herta holding Cordula, Oct. 1952.*

*Leaving Bremerhaven, Oct. 15, 1952. Günter, Helga,
Helene and Bernd are standing near the right post.*

Dining on the ship.

*Helene and Helga at
the ship's railing.*

*Arrival in the USA: with Sherry,
Kathryn, and Doc Fisher.*

The new home, New Washington, Ohio.

CPSIA information can be obtained
at www.ICGtesting.com
Printed in the USA
LVOW03s2254231117
557348LV00005B/460/P